"Sokol and Fox have produced a highly instructive and accessible workbook for youth who struggle with confidence and doubt. I enthusiastically recommend this workbook, as the authors perfectly balance the presentation of key ideas and the provision of adequate training opportunities for achieving mastery. This book will be useful as both an adjunct to therapy and a stand-alone resource."

> —**R. Trent Codd, III, EdS**, president of the Cognitive-Behavioral Therapy Center of Western North Carolina, PA behaviortherapist.com and behaviortherapist.org

"With the pressing need to help adolescents thrive in an increasingly complex world, *The Think Confident, Be Confident Workbook for Teens* serves as a much-needed resource for teens and those who care about them. Clear, engaging exercises and real-life examples guide readers to build concrete and practical strategies to face the world with strength and confidence."

> —**Torrey A. Creed, PhD**, assistant professor of psychology in psychiatry at the University of Pennsylvania Perelman School of Medicine, and coauthor of *Cognitive Therapy for Adolescents in School Settings*

D0771874

the **think confident,
be confident
workbook for teens**

activities to help you create
unshakable self-confidence
& reach your goals

LESLIE SOKOL, PhD
MARCI G FOX, PhD

Instant Help Books
An Imprint of New Harbinger Publications, Inc.

Publisher's Note

Distributed in Canada by Raincoast Books

Copyright © 2016 by Leslie Sokol and Marci G. Fox
    Instant Help Books
    An Imprint of New Harbinger Publications, Inc.
    5674 Shattuck Avenue
    Oakland, CA 94609
    www.newharbinger.com

Cover design by Amy Shoup

Acquired by Tesilya Hanauer

Edited by Clancy Drake

Library of Congress Cataloging-in-Publication Data on file

20   19   18

10 9 8 7 6 5 4 3 2

contents

Part 5: Confident Thinking

Part 6: Confident Actions

Part 7: Confident Under Pressure

Part 8: Confidence Skills At Work

foreword

The Think Confident, Be Confident Workbook for Teens is an essential and practical guide to effectively combatting an increasingly common and often harmful problem in our youth, low self-esteem. Written by two leading cognitive behavioral therapy (CBT) experts, Drs. Sokol and Fox, this much-needed, engaging interactive workbook provides teens and young adults with an in-depth understanding of confidence, why it is essential, and how self-doubt can sabotage that confidence. The helpful activities throughout the workbook help the reader gain skills directly through self-exploration and self-practice. Readers walk away with a clearer understanding of themselves as well as better tools and strategies to face the everyday world with the advantage of believing in who they are as unique individuals. The book is written in an approachable manner, and young readers will relate to both the content and the examples provided. Based on the solid principles of cognitive behavioral therapy, the reader will gain an understanding of how to eliminate unnecessary self-doubt while acquiring the most important resource of self-confidence. Armed with self-efficacy, the reader will learn to make more effective behavioral choices and maximize goal achievement. Confidence is not only built, but fortified, through skill building to last a lifetime.

Drs. Sokol and Fox were handpicked mentees of mine who have become significant leaders in the practicing, promoting, teaching, and training of cognitive behavioral therapy. I have directly trained and worked closely with them for several decades. Their explicit and clear understanding of the cognitive model and the delivery of therapy have enabled them to disseminate learning in an especially effective and captivating manner. Any teen or young adult would benefit from this wonderfully delivered evidence-based workbook. I believe it would be a great asset in any mental health professional's library as well as in any adolescent or young adult's home.

—Aaron T. Beck, MD
Professor Emeritus,
University of Pennsylvania

introduction

We're so glad you decided to check out our book. It's normal for everyone to feel insecure and experience self-doubt at times. But when you let insecurity, doubt, fear, or uncertainty win, what you really want to happen in your life doesn't happen. With confidence, you can stop getting in your own way. Self-confidence means that you believe in yourself. When you're confident, you feel good about the total package that makes up who you are: strengths, abilities, shortcomings, and all.

At different stages in your life it's common to struggle with confidence. Upsetting, confusing, or challenging situations tend to test your confidence the most. New situations may cause some self-doubt at first. In all of these moments, gaining the upper hand is the result of believing in yourself and knowing that you have the tools that can help you confidently and successfully reach your goals. Knowing that you are your own best resource means you don't have to journey alone. Fortified with self-confidence, you can get through anything and make the most of whatever life throws your way.

In this book, each activity is designed to help you understand a particular idea. You will learn more about yourself, what pushes your buttons, your self-view, and how you think, feel, and choose to act. Actively working on the activities will help you to learn, apply, and practice new skills first in the workbook and then in your everyday life. Each activity is designed to stand alone but systematically completing the entire book fortifies you to effectively face life's challenges. That way you can benefit from all the exercises even though some will be more relevant to you than others. You can refer to specific exercises to cope more effectively in the moment you most need it. This workbook functios as both a resource and an emergency distress handbook.

The exercises are designed to help you grow true confidence by squashing the needless, nasty, untrue voice of self-doubt. These exercises help you put your confidence into practice. The cognitive, emotional, and action-oriented skills arm you with tools for success. To reach for your goals, you can learn to cut out your self-defeating strategies and instead use your confidence skills in everyday life. With practice, these skills will become easier to use when you need them. The ultimate goal is to view yourself in a positive, accurate, and realistic way that prevents self-doubt, second-guessing, and comments by other people from affecting the core of who you are. Nothing and no one should be able to ruin your day. The confident you believes in you!

Leslie Sokol, PhD and Marci G. Fox, PhD

P.S. If you're a therapist interested in using this book in your work with your teen clients, we've prepared a supplemental guide for clinicians that outlines ways you can do this. Visit http://www.newharbinger.com/34831 to access it.

Part 1

Defining Confidence

1 how to define confidence

idea

Having confidence means you believe in you. Rather than facing your experiences in life with dread or apprehension, you eagerly look forward to life's challenges. You count on your own judgment. You are able to talk to anyone, because you know you are ultimately a likable person. You may dislike rejection—who doesn't—but you don't fear it. Being confident means you know you have the brain, skill, talent, experience, common sense, know-how, and competence to effectively handle whatever life throws at you. It means you think of yourself as a capable person. Having confidence means you recognize that just as others can be a resource to help you, their help does not take anything away from who you are. It means you don't have to be perfect, know everything, or have experience doing something you want to do. It means you can ask for help, learn a new skill, and make mistakes while still believing in yourself.

Confidence is very different from cockiness. When you are confident, you see yourself as a likable and capable person who can handle things on your own but also be open to benefitting from the help of others. You are able to have a positive outlook and realistically see that everyone is a unique composite of different strengths and weaknesses. Confident people are able to be happy for others when they excel because they are comfortable with themselves and do not need to make most things a real or imaginary competition. Cockiness grows from insecurity and doubt. The self-critic is always at work drawing unfair comparisons to others, inventing competitions, and feeling disconnected from truly enjoying the moment. Cocky people often make sure others are aware of their strengths even when those strengths are lacking, act like they are better than others, and refuse to recognize or work very hard to cover up their weaknesses. Cocky people tend to put other people down to make themselves feel better. Unfortunately, as much as they brag or boast, they never truly feel good or satisfied about who they are internally and often envy the confident person who is genuinely happy.

Max and Lauren

Max believes that being confident means people will like him even if he makes a mistake, messes up, or makes a fool of himself. His sense of self-worth isn't dependent on what others think or say about him; he knows at his core he is doing okay. He thinks he is basically a smart guy who can handle school, even though learning Spanish has been really hard. What makes Max confident is that he can face his weaknesses without losing sight of his overall strengths. This is the difference between Max being self-confident and Max being cocky. If Max were cocky, he would fail to see his weaknesses, think he was superior to everyone else, and give himself credit for strengths he didn't actually have.

Lauren thinks feeling confident arises from compliments or praise. She worries about what others think and say about her. She puts endless energy into her appearance, as she believes that people will think less of her if she is not looking her best. Lauren is as far from cocky as a person can be, but she does lack confidence.

Here are some examples of how others know they feel confident:

Jack knows he feels confident at home when he isn't offended by his brother's insults.

Zach knows he feels confident at school when he offers his opinion in a classroom debate.

Ally knows she feels confident with her friends when she asserts her opinion about which movie she prefers to watch.

Kyra knows she feels confident in sports and her performance when she tries out for the travel lacrosse team.

Bob knows he feels confident trying something new when he tries speaking German in public.

Salma knows she feels confident speaking in front of others when she stands up tall, looks straight at the audience, and simply shares the material she has prepared.

your turn

It is essential for you to know when you are feeling confident. The only way to gain, sustain, or grow confidence is to recognize what it is and when you experience it. Think about the situations mentioned below and see if you can recognize when you're confident.

I know I feel confident at home when I: _____

_____

I know I feel confident at school when I: _____

_____

I know I feel confident with my friends when I: _____

_____

I know I feel confident in sports or artistic performance when I: _____

_____

I know I feel confident trying something new when I: _____

_____

I know I feel confident speaking in front of others when I: _____

_____

Remind yourself of those feelings of confidence and carry them with you all day today.

more practice

Based on the examples of situations in which you know you feel confident, answer these questions:

In what ways are you already confident?

Example: Jack knows he is cool no matter what insults his brother throws at him. He is confident that he is a fun, likable, quiet guy.

_____

_____

_____

In what ways would you like to see your confidence grow?

Example: Jack would like to see his confidence on the wrestling mat grow. He questions whether he will ever be good enough to get a varsity spot.

_____

_____

_____

The Bottom Line: **I believe in me. I've got this.**

2   what does confidence feel like?

idea

Confidence is the key to success and to enjoying life. It means you count on you. Everyone gets his or her confidence shaken up periodically, especially in stressful situations. Having your confidence rattled and then restored is okay. Allowing your confidence to be damaged is not okay. When you let outside forces or your internal monologue stop you from seeing yourself in a positive, accurate, and realistic way, then self-doubt and a more negative, inaccurate view of yourself take over.

Chelsea and Austin

Chelsea wakes up feeling good about herself, tossing on her clothes, barely glancing in the mirror, and grabbing her books. She excitedly takes the stairs two steps at a time as she leaves to face her day, feeling prepared and ready. Austin, on the other hand, wakes up feeling uncomfortable in his own skin. He obsesses over what to wear and spends enormous amounts of time in front of the mirror, unhappy with what he sees. He walks slowly out of the house, dreading the day ahead, afraid of what people will think of him and how he will perform. Chelsea's story reflects self-confidence, while Austin is an example of a person with a lack of self-confidence.

Chelsea defines confidence as feeling good about herself and optimistic about her day ahead. Austin believes confidence comes from other people accepting and approving of him, which actually prevents him from feeling encouraged about his day and instead makes him feel threatened by it.

your turn

Everyone has his or her own personal experience and definition of self-confidence. The key is not to let life rattle your self-confidence. Interview four different people who you believe are confident. They could be family members, teachers, coaches, friends, community leaders, or anyone you think displays confidence. Ask each of them how they define confidence and how they know they are feeling confident. (If you need more space than the lines provided, you can download a worksheet version of this exercise at http://www.newharbinger.com/34831.)

Person 1:

How do you define confidence? _____

_____

How do you know you are feeling confident? _____

_____

Person 2:

How do you define confidence? _____

_____

How do you know you are feeling confident? _____

_____

Person 3:

How do you define confidence? _____

_____

How do you know you are feeling confident? _____

_____

Person 4:

How do you define confidence? _____

_____

How do you know you are feeling confident? _____

_____

more practice

After interviewing people, did you notice that confidence comes from more than one quality and that everyone has an individual experience of being confident? Did you gain any information that makes you want to update your definition of confidence? Write down your new view here:

_____

_____

_____

_____

_____

The Bottom Line: **Self-confidence comes from within.**

3   the confidence advantage

idea

Confidence means you believe in you. You have put your faith in you and not someone else. You have your own back. In response to any situation, you make yourself responsible for your thoughts, feelings, and behaviors. You recognize that you can be in charge of what you think, feel, or do without being defiant or uncooperative. When you depend on yourself, you are able to grow your competence and your likability. You define yourself rather than waiting for others to define you. Other people can't ruin your day, make you feel bad, or stress you out. Others' actions or opinions can still disappoint you or cause you pain, and life can feel tough, but that doesn't have to affect your core. When a friend doesn't include you or you don't make the team, your feelings of desirability and competence remain intact.

In this way, having confidence means you don't feel threatened by life. You know that when someone doesn't like you or want to date you, or is just giving you a hard time, it doesn't mean anything about your overall desirability or likability. Similarly, if you make a mistake, don't know something, or cannot quite master a skill, it doesn't mean you are not capable. Knowing you are a desirable and capable person means you are confident.

Arjun

One week, Arjun bombed a test and was feeling a little demoralized. Instead of giving up, he became determined to do better and to seek out all the help he could get. His confidence helped him dig in and do better on his next test. Later, Arjun tried to get a group of people to go to a concert with him, but no one was interested. Instead of feeling rejected or friendless, he accepted that no one wanted to spend the money or make the effort to go this time. So he continued looking for concerts, knowing one would eventually appeal to his friends.

your turn

It's possible to face difficult situations and not let them get the best of you. Here are some phrases that you can say to yourself the next time you experience a negative situation or things don't turn out the way you want.

Write the difficult situation here:

_____

_____

Try telling yourself:

- Don't give up: dig in and try again.

- I can figure out the help I need and seek it out.

- This one situation is not the big picture.

What else might you tell yourself?

_____

_____

_____

more practice

Recall a situation in which things did not go your way socially or academically, or in which you did not perform as well as you wanted, yet you did not let it defeat you.

Example: *I wanted to go to a school football game, but no one wanted to go with me.*

Name a situation. What happened? Write the details here:

_____

_____

What stopped the situation from getting the best of you? Were you aware of how you were thinking about it at the time?

Example: *Everyone was too tired from studying for finals to go. It wasn't me.*

_____

_____

Write down your confidence-boosting thoughts here:

Example: *I could have let the fact that no one wanted to go make me feel like I don't have any friends, but I didn't jump to that false conclusion.*

_____

_____

_____

Did you learn anything from your confidence-boosting thoughts?

Example: *Recognize the real reason behind people's choices.*

_____

_____

_____

The Bottom Line: **Don't blow things out of proportion.**

4   without confidence

idea

Without confidence, negativity gets the best of you. It influences your perspective, and you wind up drawing conclusions that don't jive with the truth. You start second-guessing yourself and your decisions, allowing anxiety and even despair to sink in.

Robby

Robby was getting ready to go out and meet his friends. He felt good about the way he had dressed and was looking forward to hanging out with everyone. Robby got into his friend's car and the friend started giving him a hard time about his shirt. Robby started to worry that he made a bad choice and that other people would say or think the same thing. That's when Robby noticed he was feeling uncomfortably nervous.

your turn

Confidence means that you look at each situation in your life objectively, so you see the big picture rather than getting stuck in a specific moment in time. When you lack confidence, you get stuck in specific moments, taking any criticism to mean that you're not okay as a person.

If friends say they liked your hair better before you cut it, without confidence you might think:

- *I ruined my appearance.*

- *This is a disaster; I have to try to fix it immediately.*

- *My hair will never look good again.*

- _____

With confidence, you might think:

- *I like this haircut; who cares what anyone else thinks.*

- *This is a lousy haircut, but luckily it will grow out.*

- *This is a bad haircut, but my hair is not the only thing going for me.*

- _____

Imagine you are giving a speech in class and you mispronounce a word. Without confidence, you might think:

- *I made a fool of myself.*

- *This is a nightmare; I've destroyed my grade.*

- *No one will forget this; I'm going to hear about it all day.*

- _____

With confidence, you might think:

- *I did a pretty good job, even if I did flub that one word.*

- *I wish I hadn't messed up that word, but no big deal.*

- *I bet no one even cares, or let alone noticed, that I mispronounced one word.*

- _____

more practice

Practice the confidence advantage. Pick a specific situation this week that you are apprehensive about facing and use your confidence to go for your desired outcome. Write out the specific situation and your confident thoughts. Afterward, write about what you gained by pushing yourself to take action.

Specific situation:

Example: *I want to try yoga.*

_____

_____

Your confident thoughts:

Example: *Yoga is something I really want to try, so I should go for it. I don't have to be good at it when I'm starting out. It's a class, which means someone is going to be teaching me what to do.*

_____

_____

What you gained by pushing yourself to go for it:

Example: *I could have let my old way of thinking, which is self-defeating rather than confident, talk me out of doing something I really want to try. Now I know that by pushing myself I won't miss out on future opportunities. I feel good about myself because I went for it and tried yoga.*

_____

_____

_____

Pick two situations you will need to face this week that you are apprehensive about and use your confidence to go for it. Write out the specific situation and the confident thoughts. Afterward, write what you gained by pushing yourself to take action.

Situation 1: _____

_____

Write down your "with confidence" thoughts here:

_____

_____

Write down what you gained by pushing yourself to go for it:

_____

_____

_____

Situation 2: _____

_____

Write down your confident thoughts here:

_____

_____

Write down what you gained by pushing yourself to go for it:

_____

_____

_____

The Bottom Line: **Use the advantage of confidence to go for it.**

Part 2

Defining Doubt

5   what is self-doubt?

idea

Self-doubt is a harsh critic to have sitting on your shoulder. Rather than making a fair call about a situation, it defines you with an extremely negative label. You can't see yourself in a realistic and accurate way; instead, you focus on yourself in a negative way.

Chandni

Sometimes Chandni wakes up feeling so good about herself. The day in front of her is clear and she's ready to start it. Other days, she wakes up riddled with self-doubt that makes everything feel hard. Chandni doesn't like the way she feels in her clothes or the way she looks in the mirror. As she travels to school, Chandni feels overwhelmed and worries about her schoolwork. She second-guesses every decision she makes, from what she should eat to how to answer a question on a test. In her head, she hears herself saying: "I'm not good enough." All this thinking clouds her mind with doubt and makes it really hard to concentrate.

your turn

Take this doubt quiz to see whether you experience self-doubt. Check all the statements that apply to you.

Have you often...

_____ felt down?

_____ been self-critical?

_____ been uncertain?

_____ been insecure?

_____ been hard on yourself?

_____ beat yourself up mentally?

_____ second-guessed yourself?

_____ taken the blame when there were other factors that also played a role?

_____ taken a neutral situation and turned it into an example of your shortcoming?

_____ taken things personally?

_____ given up rather than tried?

_____ believed in others more than in yourself?

_____ taken a weakness and let it define you?

_____ avoided something you cared about or wanted to do?

_____ let your thoughts paralyze your efforts?

_____ not bothered sticking up for yourself?

_____ let someone talk you into something you knew wasn't okay to do?

_____ let someone talk you into something you didn't want to do?

_____ gone along with something that your gut told you was wrong?

_____ felt guilty, even when you are not at fault?

If you answered yes to any of these questions, then you've experienced self-doubt. Here is a scale that will help you know how much you are held back by self-doubt.

0–2 checkmarks: You rarely experience self-doubt

3–7 checkmarks: You often experience self-doubt

8–20 checkmarks: You consistently experience self-doubt

more practice

It is helpful to recognize when your self-doubting thoughts have been triggered. Self-doubt can lead you to jump to the wrong conclusion, to change or question a good decision, or to do something you later regret. When doubt is in charge, you feel bad about yourself and can make poor choices.

This week, try to notice when you experience self-doubt. Record each time it arises. Use the quiz in this exercise (available for download at http://www.newharbinger .com/34831) to recognize how self-doubt expressed itself.

Situation: _____

_____

Self-doubt expressed: _____

_____

Situation: _____

_____

Self-doubt expressed: _____

_____

At the end of the week, look at your record. Do you notice any patterns? Are there certain circumstances in which doubt tends to show up the most? Write down your observations here.

_____

_____

The Bottom Line: **Look out for your doubt.**

6 understand what you value

idea

What you value is directly connected with the actions that make you feel good about yourself. If accomplishments, such as getting good grades, performing on the field, or getting something done, matter most to you, then you can consider yourself more achievement-oriented. On the other hand, if being social by caring about others, being a good friend, or being liked by others matters more to you, then you can consider yourself social-oriented. Are you achievement- or social-oriented or both? Let's find out.

Nikki and Mario

Early Monday morning, sign-up sheets were posted for the required community service day off campus. Nikki was the first one to put her name on the list. Even though she was hoping her friends would pick her same choice, her achievement-oriented nature led her to pick her desired activity rather than waiting to see her friends' choices. Mario, on the other hand, being more social-oriented, waited all day to see what his friends signed up for before adding his name to their choice—which happened to be his least favorite.

your turn

Take these quizzes to find out if you're achievement- or social-oriented. Check all the statements that apply to you.

Are you achievement-oriented?

_____ I set goals and strive to reach them.

_____ My self-worth comes from my performance in school, athletics, extracurricular activities, or whatever it is I want to do.

_____ If I have to choose between doing what I want to do or an opportunity to be social, I typically choose what I want to do.

_____ I prefer to be considered capable or smart rather than nice or friendly.

_____ I take my social life for granted and place more importance on working hard or doing what I want.

_____ I define myself by what I do, not by how much people like me.

_____ I like competition.

_____ I perform better when I'm competing.

_____ I enjoy doing what I like, even if no one wants to do it with me.

_____ My biggest priority is getting things done.

_____ I like having the freedom to do what I want.

Are you social-oriented?

_____ I feel that being loved or accepted is better than accomplishing a task.

_____ I believe it's more important to be viewed as kind or caring than smart.

_____ I care about what other people think of me.

_____ I tend to pick what others want to do over what I want to do.

_____ It's more important to me to be liked than to do what seems right for me.

_____ I find it easier to go with the flow than to step on anyone's toes.

_____ I don't like competition and am likely to fall apart under pressure to compete.

_____ I am more likely to be concerned about what others think when I choose my clothes, cut my hair, or act goofy.

_____ My goals are easily swayed by the influence of others.

_____ My self-worth comes from my social success.

_____ I'd rather be with my friends than do any given activity.

What did you learn?

How many items did you check on the achievement-oriented quiz: _____

How many items did you check on the social-oriented quiz: _____

Are you more achievement-oriented or social-oriented? _____

Or are you equally high on both scales? _____

more practice

Now that you are aware of what you value most, whether it's achievement or being social or a mix of both, you can begin to see how it affects your day-to-day decisions. Specifically, look at the choices you make when you are pulled in different directions and see if you pick the achievement-oriented path or the social one.

Example

Situation: *A bunch of your friends are hanging out together. You would like to go to the basketball game but no one else wants to go.*

Dilemma: *Hang with your friends and miss out on the game or go to the game and leave your friends.*

Choice: *Go to the game.*

Achievement __x__ or Social _____

Now it's your turn to identify a situation and choose how to respond.

Situation: _____

_____

Dilemma: _____

_____

Choice: _____

Achievement _____ or Social _____

Make note of how your achievement and/or social concerns affect your decision making:

The Bottom Line: **Pay attention to the choices you make and have the courage to pick what you really want to do.**

31

7   what bothers you?

idea

What is really important to you determines the types of situations and events that are likely to upset you. The achievement-oriented person is likely to stress when performance-related situations are not going as planned or efforts are thwarted in some way. Additionally, when independence, freedom, or mobility is threatened, distress is likely to follow. On the other hand, a more social-oriented person will experience more stress when situations cause rejection, arguments, or exclusion.

Yasmin

Yasmin is looking forward to a concert. She loves the band, and a couple of her friends bought tickets with her months ago; the tickets were expensive, so she had to scramble to find the money. The problem is that her new boyfriend keeps texting her, trying to get her to hang out with him instead. She can't believe he is pressuring her not to go, and the thought of missing the concert is way more distressing to her than her boyfriend's upset, so she's going anyway. If Yasmin had been more social-oriented she might have missed the concert for the sake of her relationship.

your turn

Take this test to figure out what bothers you. Determine your feelings about each of the following statements and circle yes or no to indicate whether it is true for you or not.

You are bothered by…

1. criticism, real or imagined, regarding your performance	YES	NO
2. rejection, real or imagined	YES	NO
3. feeling as if you have no control	YES	NO
4. disagreement with another person	YES	NO
5. a loss of independence	YES	NO
6. being left out or excluded	YES	NO
7. encountering difficulty in achieving a goal	YES	NO
8. someone being upset with you	YES	NO
9. being told, rather than asked, to do something	YES	NO
10. feeling awkward in a social situation	YES	NO
11. not living up to your own expectations	YES	NO
12. criticism, real or imagined, regarding social interaction	YES	NO
13. difficulty completing what you want to do	YES	NO
14. not having calls or texts returned	YES	NO

Look at all the odd numbers: 1, 3, 5, 7, 9, 11, 13

How many yeses did you circle? _____

Look at all the even numbers: 2, 4, 6, 8, 10, 12, 14

How many yeses did you circle? _____

A higher score of odd numbers means achievement-oriented situations matter to you and when they don't go your way, you feel upset.

A higher score of even numbers means social situations matter to you and when they don't go your way, you feel upset.

An equally high score of both even and odd numbers means that both achievement-oriented and social situations matter to you. When situations of either type don't go your way, you feel upset.

When you feel upset, is the cause more achievement-oriented, social-oriented, or both?

What can you conclude about what bothers you during your day?

_____

_____

_____

more practice

Make a list of things that upset you this week and note whether it was achievement- or social-oriented.

Event	Achievement or Social

The Bottom Line: **Be on the lookout for what kinds of situations push your buttons.**

8   give doubt a name

idea

We all feel some insecurity inside and the nasty name we call ourselves is simply the label we put on that insecurity. Some of us have only one nasty name for ourselves while others have tons of names.

Emily and Drew

Emily's lacrosse team finally won a game after four consecutive losses. Instead of praising them, their coach told them, "Don't let this win go to your heads. You girls are still not 'good enough' and the extra practice times are still on the schedule this week." Emily went home, looked at her pile of homework and thought, "It's true, I'm not good enough on the field or in school." Emily has a habit of calling herself, "Not good enough."

Drew arrived at his friend's house to pick up the crew and head to a movie. As friends piled into his car, they told Drew that he just didn't have any sense of style. Drew looked at his shorts and shirt and thought, "What's wrong with how I'm dressed?" At the movie theater, they ran into some girls they knew. While the others were flirting away, Drew stood awkwardly, thinking, "I have no sense of style." Drew has a habit of calling himself, "Uncool."

your turn

Here are examples of what those nasty names might be:

Airhead	Fraud	Not good enough	Undesirable
Absentminded	Helpless	Outcast	Unimaginative
Average	Hideous	Pathetic	Unimportant
Awkward	Hotheaded	Plain	Uninteresting
Boring	Idiot	Quiet	Unlikable
Bad	Inadequate	Shy	Unlovable
Difficult	Incapable	Slow	Unwanted
Disgusting	Incompetent	Spaz	Unworthy
Don't measure up	Inferior	Stupid	Useless
Dumb	Insignificant	Ugly	Weak
Dumbass	Lazy	Unattractive	Weird
Failure	Loser	Uncool	Weirdo
Fat	Moody	Uncoordinated	Worthless

Look through this list a second time and circle the names you call yourself when you are being hard on yourself. Are there any names you use that are not on the list? If so, write them down here:

_____ _____ _____

more practice

It is important to recognize the nasty names you call yourself and know that just because you, or anyone else, calls you that name doesn't make it an accurate description.

1. What are your self-doubt labels—the negative ways you describe yourself, such as "I'm an incompetent loser" or "I'm an airhead"?

   Write down your self-doubt labels:

   _____

   _____

   _____

2. Are these labels one-hundred percent true across the board, in every single situation?

   Circle one answer: YES   NO

   If you answered no, you are ready to begin viewing yourself in a more accurate way.

3. Whether you think your labels are completely true or not, write down five examples of ways your doubt labels don't fit.

Examples: *I aced my biology test.*

I found the keys I thought I had lost.

A friend called to ask for my help with solving a personal issue.

I made my family a delicious dinner.

I finished all my homework in record time.

_____

_____

_____

_____

_____

No one's self-doubt labels offer a complete picture of who they are. Even if they are not particularly good at any one thing, no one is one-hundred percent not good enough.

The Bottom Line: **Beware of those nasty names you call yourself and know they are never absolutely true.**

9   when life is hard

idea

It's normal to feel good about yourself when things are going well. When life is going your way, you aren't likely to experience self-doubt or inflict nasty name-calling on yourself. However, when you're experiencing difficulties and life isn't going your way, you may not feel as good about yourself. You are more likely to have lots of self-doubt, which affects your confidence.

Butch

Butch had only had his driving permit for a few weeks when he was driving to school with his mother in the passenger seat. Butch thought things were going well and felt pretty confident as he picked up speed. He noticed the traffic ahead coming to a complete stop and he calmly pressed the brakes and stopped the car. Suddenly, he felt impact from the car behind them as it slammed into his car. Butch's confidence was shattered because he automatically thought he'd done something wrong and that the accident was his fault. His negative belief that he was not competent was confirmed and he questioned whether he would ever drive well. Butch's good mood sank and for the rest of the day he saw only his shortcomings.

your turn

Recall a recent situation when things didn't go your way. Did doubt take over? Did you get down on yourself and end up calling yourself nasty names? In the examples below, notice how doubt operates.

Situation: Your classmate is having a party and you didn't get an invite.

Does doubt rule? If so, you may think any of the following things. Feel free to come up with examples of your own.

- *He probably doesn't like me.*

- *I'm not cool enough to hang out with this group.*

- *I'm always on the outside.*

- _____

- _____

You might call yourself any of the following names. If any nasty names come to mind that you actually call yourself, add them to the list.

- Loser

- Weirdo

- Awkward

- Uncool

- _____

- _____

Situation: You bombed a test.

Does doubt rule? If so, you may think any of the following things. Feel free to come up with examples of your own.

- *I will never understand this stuff.*

- *Why keep trying? I'll fail anyway.*

- *Everyone thinks I'm dumb.*

- _____

- _____

You might call yourself any of the following names. If any nasty names come to mind that you actually call yourself, add them to the list.

- Stupid

- Incompetent

- Failure

- Average

- _____

- _____

Situation: You had a fight with your friend.

Does doubt rule? If so, you may think any of the following things. Feel free to come up with examples of your own.

- *I really messed up.*

- *Our relationship is over for good.*

- *She or he will never get over this.*

- _____

- _____

You might call yourself any of the following names. If any nasty names come to mind that you actually call yourself, add them to the list.

- Unwanted

- Loser

- Not good enough

- Moody

- _____

- _____

more practice

The next time you face a difficult situation, things just don't go your way, or circumstances don't work out the way you were hoping for, notice whether self-doubt shows up. If you notice doubt, try to catch the nasty name you call yourself and make note of it.

Situation: _____

_____

Did self-doubt show up? Circle one answer: YES   NO

If yes, what were the nasty names you called yourself?

_____

_____

_____

The Bottom Line: **Stuff happens; I don't have to degrade myself as a result.**

doubt doesn't define you

idea

Rather than letting self-doubt define you, recognize that you are made up of many pieces. You are composed of a multitude of qualities that make you unique. You are a package, not any single item. Expand your self-definition by increasing your awareness of characteristics that define who you are.

Jack, Allison, Mia, Ryan, Mike, and Caroline

Jack says, "I'm not an athlete—in fact, I'm not even coordinated. But I'm the smart one."

Allison says, "I'm not a brainiac, but Spanish and art are my things."

Mia says, "I don't have a great body, but I have a friendly face and an upbeat personality."

Ryan says, "I'm not all that smart, but I'm a really good football player and I'm unstoppable at video games."

Mike says, "I'm awkward, but I'm actually really funny and make a good friend."

Caroline says, "I'm shy, but I'm an excellent listener."

your turn

Here are some assets and qualities that might define you:

Animal lover	Foodie	Loud	Petite
Artistic	Forgetful	Loving	Problem solver
Athletic	Friendly	Low-key	Put together well
Awkward	Funny	Loyal	Quick
Baker	Gamer	Math whiz	Quiet
Big	Generous	Mechanical	Reader
Book-smart	Griller	Movie watcher	Reliable
Caring	Gritty	Multilingual	Responsible
Chef	Hairstyle	Multitasker	Scientist
Considerate	Happy	Musical	Short
Coordinated	Hardworking	Nails	Singer
Creative	Helper	Neat	Smile
Curious	High-maintenance	Nonathletic	Street-smart
Dancer	Hot-tempered	On the ball	Strong
Determined	Interested	Open-minded	Stylish
Disorganized	Introverted	Optimist	Talkative
Energetic	Kind	Organized	Tall
Engineer	Leader	Outdoorsy	Thoughtful
Entrepreneurial	Lean	Outgoing	Worker
Eye color	Listener	Patient	Writer

Fill in this jigsaw puzzle with all of the qualities that make up you.

I AM...

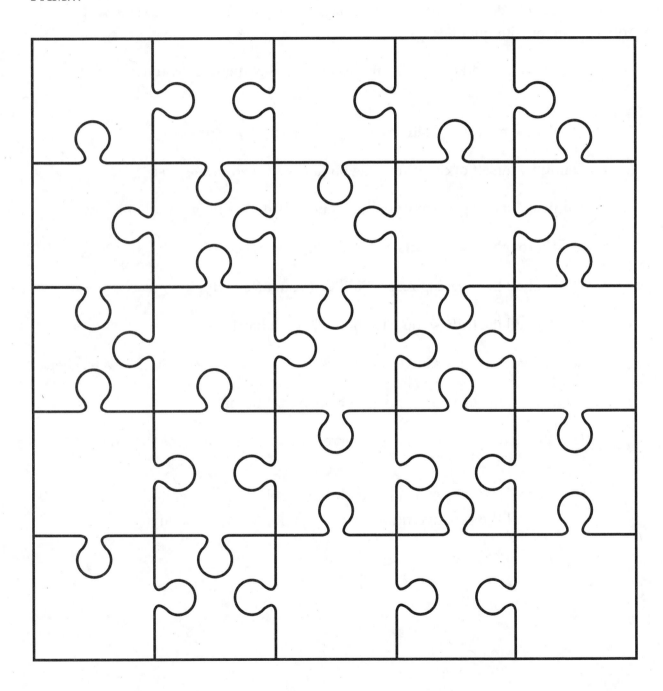

more practice

Expand your confidence by continuing to add to the puzzle. Here are some ways to collect more of your qualities.

- Interview a friend or relative and ask them what qualities you have that they like.

- Think of something positive someone said about you recently.

- Remind yourself of compliments you have received in the past.

- Think about any problems you have successfully faced or handled lately.

- Read through texts, e-mails, or cards you have received.

- Think of all the ongoing responsibilities you have and take care of.

- Think of all the things you have done that felt hard.

- Remind yourself of positive comments you received from a coach or a teacher.

- Look around your room for objects you are proud of.

- Think of some project you have worked on or something you created.

The Bottom Line: **Your self-doubt labels can be negated by all the positive qualities that make up who you are.**

Part 3

Where Does Doubt Come From?

11 events can play a role

idea

How you think about yourself and what you believe about yourself don't come out of the blue. They come from the way you think about life situations and experiences, especially difficult ones. If you assign external events or messages too much importance, it's easy to let them convince you that some negative label is true. When you personalize external things, self-doubt can develop.

Porscha

Porscha's parents are divorced. Both of them seem too busy with their lives to have time for her and she doesn't feel important to them. Porscha thinks her parents' divorce is messing with her head. Porscha finds walking up to her friends really difficult because she worries that she might say something that upsets them or that they won't want to hang out with her. Sometimes she thinks it would be easier to just walk the other way and pretend she doesn't see them. She believes she doesn't matter, that she isn't important.

your turn

Porscha uses her external experiences to indicate something negative about her personally. Her parents' divorce and behavior give her a strong, steady message that she doesn't matter. She looks for ways to confirm this view, taking note of whenever she feels unwanted and concluding that the people she loves don't care much for her.

Take time to think about how situations from your past negatively affect the way you see yourself now. Have you lived through any of the following experiences? Note that this is not an exhaustive list. You may have faced a situation that you don't find here.

Did you experience a move?

Did it take you longer than other kids to learn to crawl, walk, or talk?

Did you change schools?

Did you have to switch classes?

Did you have to change levels within a specific subject?

Did your teacher insist on meeting with your parents?

Did you experience any health issues or illnesses?

Were you held back in school?

Did you get into trouble in school?

Did you ever get into trouble with law enforcement?

Did your parents separate or divorce?

Did you have an upsetting experience with your siblings?

Did you experience a tough fight with a friend?

Has something traumatic happened to someone you know?

Were you ever at fault in some type of accident?

Did something painful happen in your school or community?

Were you exposed to a natural disaster?

Did you not make the cut on a team, in a show, or for a club?

Did you try out for a part or run for a position and it didn't work out?

Did you put yourself out there for someone and it didn't turn out well for you?

Was there something you were not included in or wished you could be a part of?

Did a romantic interest not seem to work out?

Did you experience a breakup?

Did you not get a job?

Did you get fired?

Have you faced death?

Was there extreme conflict or violence in your life?

Have you faced abuse or trauma?

Have you been bullied or teased?

Has your family faced money problems?

Have you faced housing problems?

Have you ever been injured in a serious accident?

Do you have ill or impaired siblings or parents?

Have you had any serious injuries?

Have you drawn meaning about yourself from any of these situations? Did they play a role in shaping your self-doubt?

Write down a situation from your past or present:

_____

_____

Did this situation trigger doubt? Circle one answer: YES   NO

Did it shift the way you think about yourself? Circle one answer: YES   NO

Describe how it affected you:

_____

_____

Did you label yourself with a doubt-name? If so, what are you calling yourself?

_____

more practice

Don't let any external situation imply something personal about you or define you. It's like taking repeat off your song list and playing the full album so that you see yourself fairly. When you play your life all the way through, you will recognize that there are 365 days in a year with 3,600 minutes per day. Lots and lots of stuff happens in that time. The next time your interpretation of a situation triggers self-doubt, catch the nasty label you are giving yourself and replace it with a big picture, drawn from the jigsaw puzzle that makes up you.

Example

Situation: Brian's first girlfriend breaks up with him and then starts dating his friend.

Brian's self-doubt label: I'm average. No wonder she wants someone better.

Brian's broader perspective: I have things going for me. I'm smart, funny, and a good guy. Maybe she just likes hanging out with him more than me. It's true that they both love to make music and that's just not my thing.

Situation: _____

_____

Self-doubt label: _____

A broader perspective: _____

_____

_____

The Bottom Line: **Life experiences matter, but events do not define you.**

idea

Self-doubt can develop from messages and interactions with important people in your life. You can assign an offhand comment more meaning than it deserves, just like being called mean names in the heat of an argument can bring you down more than it should. What people call you, what you think they are calling you, or what you suspect they think about you is not the problem. The problem occurs when you let the names you hear, or imagine, define you. Even a random encounter with a stranger could negatively affect your self-view, if you let it. The most important thing you can do for yourself is be your own fair judge.

Lily

Lily puts so much time and energy into studying. Her brother is able to go out and do lots of other things while she is stuck with her books. Lily often thinks she is not as smart as her brother and that other people seem to have it easier. On a good day, she realizes that she is a good student; however, on the tougher days, she calls herself an idiot and wonders how long it'll take before her friends and teachers realize it, too. During these moments her mood sinks and she gets very self-critical. She believes her brother doesn't struggle with school because he is the smart one. And it doesn't help that he gets much better grades than she does, which teachers give her a hard time about.

your turn

When Lily hears people say that her brother is "the smart one," a comparison is being made that indicates she is not "the smart one." Therefore, she concludes that she must be dumb. Most likely, that's not true. But you can see how she heard that message, took it to heart, and let it chip away at her sense of self. Have you heard messages that negatively affect the way you see yourself? Who said them and what were they?

The table that follows contains a list of potential sources for negative messages you hear. Can you recall anyone on the list saying something you heard in a way that negatively affected you? If so, identify the messages you heard and the nasty doubt labels they inspired.

	Message	Doubt Label
Parents		
Siblings		
Relatives		
Neighbors		
Coaches		
Teachers		
Religious officials		
Friends		
Club leaders		
Babysitters		
Boyfriends		
Girlfriends		
Classmates		
Peers		
Employers		
Strangers		
You		

more practice

Who contributed to your self-doubt? Think of each person and decide what percentage of your self-doubt he or she contributed to. Then divide the circle offered here into a pie chart with proportions that reflect the extent to which each person has contributed to the doubt you now hold about yourself. Don't forget to put yourself in there. If you find it hard to fill out the pie chart, then your doubt probably isn't getting the best of you.

The Bottom Line: **Just because you hear it doesn't mean it's true.**

idea

The beliefs that you have about yourself today are the result of your personal interpretations of your yesterdays. Events, social interactions, and messages—internal and external—are seeds for both your self-doubt and your confidence. Even as a baby, you faced the external world with your own temperament and genetic makeup. Were you the baby who needed to fall asleep on someone's chest or the one who easily went to sleep alone in a crib? Did you venture off to explore and push boundaries or did you sit and contentedly observe your environment? As life experiences accumulate, your perceptions of those experiences and the way others interpret them for you shape the lens you see yourself through. Identifying those experiences, examining them, and questioning your old conclusions can help you remove obstructive self-doubt and build your confidence. Confidence results from learning to look at life experiences accurately so that you can view yourself in a positive and realistic way.

Paul

Paul's mom told him that he was trouble before he was even born. She had to take medication to prevent an early delivery and an arduous birth left him with a dislocated shoulder. Paul cried all the time and never wanted to be put down. He has been a night owl from day one, which makes functioning in the morning tough. All of this has led the family to label Paul "the difficult one." In class and on the football field, he finds it hard to pay attention. His teachers are always complaining about his lack of focus, and his coach yells at him for it. All of this has convinced Paul that he is difficult.

your turn

Fill out this life timeline. For each time period, identify significant and insignificant memories that contribute to your self-image. You might know the information already, or you might have to ask other people.

Here's an example, from Natalie's life:

In Mom's Belly: Mom says her pregnancy was horrible. She was sick all the time and was prescribed bed rest with limited activity. Mom complains about this, even to this day.

My Birth: Mom says her recovery from the C-section caused her to be stuck at home for even longer.

Infant: Mom says I was very demanding and wanted to be held all the time.

Toddler: Mom says I had a lot of ear infections, which often compromised playdates and activities.

Ages 3–6: Mom says I always seemed to need her when she was busy trying to do her own thing.

Ages 7–10: Mom worried that I didn't have enough friends because I spent a lot of time alone in my own world.

Ages 11–13: Mom was always harassing me to join an activity.

Ages 14–17: Mom and I fight all the time. She regularly says she is disappointed in me.

Ages 18 and Up: Not there yet, but I know Mom will pressure me to join a sorority.

Now it's your turn to record data on your timeline.

In Mom's Belly: _____

_____

My Birth: _____

_____

Infant: _____

_____

Toddler: _____

_____

Ages 3–6: _____

_____

Ages 7–10: _____

_____

Ages 11–13: _____

_____

Ages 14–17: _____

_____

Ages 18 and Up: _____

_____

more practice

Look at your timeline. For each time period, ask yourself if you let something contribute to your doubt label. If so, what nasty name did you call yourself as a result? Try to see if there is one or possibly more nasty doubt labels connecting all of these events. It may be the same one, or you may have a lot of different names.

In Natalie's example, what are the doubt labels she might call herself?

_____   _____   _____

Did you consider any of these labels: unlikable, undesirable, insignificant, shy, unimportant, unlovable, unwanted? Her doubt label could be any one of these, or many others.

Here is a list of the doubt labels you might call yourself. In Activity 8, these were called "nasty names." They are also sources of self-doubt and it is helpful to consider where they might come from. Use your timeline to reflect on your life memories, and then circle the doubt labels you created based on your life experiences.

Airhead	Inadequate	Unattractive
Absentminded	Incapable	Uncool
Average	Incompetent	Uncoordinated
Awkward	Inferior	Undesirable
Boring	Insignificant	Unimaginative
Bad	Lazy	Unimportant
Difficult	Loser	Uninteresting
Disgusting	Moody	Unlikable
Don't measure up	Not good enough	Unlovable
Dumb	Outcast	Unwanted
Dumbass	Pathetic	Unworthy
Failure	Plain	Useless
Fat	Quiet	Weak
Fraud	Shy	Weird
Helpless	Slow	Weirdo
Hideous	Spaz	Worthless
Hotheaded	Stupid	Other:
Idiot	Ugly	_____

The Bottom Line: **Your view of life experiences shapes your doubt.**

Part 4

Build Self-Confidence

14 your confidence path

idea

Your history and the way you interpret it play major roles in shaping your self-doubt and your self-confidence. Positive feedback influences confidence. Listening for and embracing positive messages lays a foundation for the growth of self-confidence. Think back to positive experiences throughout your life. Use these memories as opportunities to draw objectively positive, realistic, and accurate views of yourself. Examples of positive experiences include: praise, goal attainment, and achievements in any area, whether academic, athletic, social, or artistic. Positive feedback can be loud and clear, subtle, or perceived. Being told you are the MVP of the game is a loud and clear message, while it's subtler to receive a pat on the back or have someone whisper, "Nice game," in your ear.

Chase

When Chase was seven years old, his parents enrolled him in a karate program. He was the smallest and one of the least experienced kids in the program, but the instructor encouraged him to compete in a major competition anyway. The instructor assured Chase that he would be competing against kids at the same level and size. To Chase's surprise, he won the competition and went home with a trophy that was bigger than him. Plus, his picture was posted front and center on the karate program's website. Chase walked away from this experience knowing that he had it in him to be a winner. Two years later, when Chase's soccer coach asked him to fill in as goalie, a position he didn't want to play, he fearlessly stepped up. Every time he blocked a goal, Chase confirmed that he had it in him to succeed.

your turn

Fill out your life timeline from a positive perspective. For each time period, identify significant and insignificant memories of events that contributed to your positive self-image. You might know the information already, or you might have to ask other people.

Here's an example from Natalie's life:

In Mom's Belly: Mom says she didn't gain too much weight with my pregnancy.

My Birth: Mom says she has fond memories of the way Dad cried when I was born.

Infant: Mom says I was a beautiful baby and that she loved dressing me in all sorts of cute outfits.

Toddler: Mom says she appreciated how she could set me in a corner and get lots of things done while I quietly played by myself.

Ages 3–6: Mom says I wasn't a particularly active kid, so our house was less crazy then it was after my brother came along.

Ages 7–10: Mom liked that I rarely complained and was happy and willing to go to school.

Ages 11–13: Mom says I never had any academic issues in school.

Ages 14–17: Mom says she appreciates that she never has to nag me to get my homework done.

Age 18 and Up: Not there yet.

Now it's your turn to record your data on the timeline.

In Mom's Belly: _____

_____

My Birth: _____

_____

Infant: _____

_____

Toddler: _____

_____

Ages 3–6: _____

_____

Ages 7–10: _____

_____

Ages 11–13: _____

_____

Ages 14–17: _____

_____

Ages 18 and Up: _____

_____

more practice

Look back at your timeline. For each time period, ask yourself if you let something influence a positive view of yourself. Try to see the positive view you gained from your history.

In Natalie's case, what are examples of positive labels she might call herself?

_____

Did you consider lovable, likable, appealing, funny, or serene? The positive labels she might call herself could be any of these or many others.

On the next page is a list of self-confident beliefs. Reflect on your own timeline and circle all the positive labels that you heard.

Adequate	Diplomatic	Reliable
Admired	Funny	Serene
Appealing	Good enough	Shrewd
Athletic	Helpful	Significant
Attractive	Hip	Smart
Brainiac	Important	Social
Built	Interesting	Street-smart
Calculating	Likable	Strong
Capable	Lovable	Stylish
Competent	Measuring up	Suave
Composed	Nice	Successful
Cool	Normal	Trendy
Coordinated	Outgoing	Useful
Creative	Popular	Wanted
Crafty	Powerful	Winning
Desirable	Quiet	Worthy

The Bottom Line: **Recall the positive experiences in your life and own them.**

name your confidence 15

idea

Positive experiences grow your confident view of yourself when you make clear and helpful conclusions about those experiences. When you do well at anything, experience success, or receive praise, compliments, and positive feedback, it's crucial to recognize that this information means something. The meaning you assign to these positive experiences can build a foundation for feeling capable and liked. Knowing you have the capacity to succeed, through achievement and social situations, fortifies you against life's challenges.

Carly

Last year, Carly ran for student government president and was surprised when many of her friends worked on her campaign. When she won, she thought she must truly have what it takes for so many people to want to support her. Although this year has been hard academically, Carly created an awesome experiment for the science fair, which helped her recognize how capable she is.

your turn

Here is the list of self-confident beliefs. Circle all the ones that ring true.

Adequate	Diplomatic	Reliable
Admired	Funny	Serene
Appealing	Good enough	Shrewd
Athletic	Helpful	Significant
Attractive	Hip	Smart
Brainiac	Important	Social
Built	Interesting	Street-smart
Calculating	Likable	Strong
Capable	Lovable	Stylish
Competent	Measuring up	Suave
Composed	Nice	Successful
Cool	Normal	Trendy
Coordinated	Outgoing	Useful
Creative	Popular	Wanted
Crafty	Powerful	Winning
Desirable	Quiet	Worthy

more practice

Look at the labels you circled and, with a different color, circle any additional positive labels that others have called you, even if you don't see yourself that way.

Then survey friends and family and ask them if any of these confidence labels fit you. Circle those in a third color.

Notice how many positive beliefs about you exist. Write down all the positive names you have collected here:

_____   _____

_____   _____

_____   _____

_____   _____

_____   _____

_____   _____

_____   _____

Each day, take time to reflect on each of these positive labels and consider how you can use this information to grow the confident you.

The Bottom Line: **Everyone has positive labels;
find yours and pay attention to them.**

16 confident vs. cocky

idea

Self-confidence results from seeing yourself in a positive, accurate, and rational way while still being aware of your weaknesses. Cockiness is something completely different. It comes from a falsely elevated view of yourself that doesn't have any objective facts to back it up. Cockiness means you have lost sight of your weaknesses and view yourself as better than everyone else. Contrarily, while with confidence you recognize when you are particularly good at something or have an exceptional talent, you also know many others share your gifts.

Jessica and Jake

Jessica is a skilled violinist and was appalled when the orchestra leader gave first chair to a student Jessica believed was not nearly as good. Jessica believes she is a superior writer and assumed her essay would be chosen for the school paper only to be shocked when it wasn't.

Jake is the go-to man for help with math homework since he is especially talented in the subject. He is also not afraid to ask for help when he faces a particularly challenging problem. Jake scored two goals in yesterday's soccer game and still happily cheered to support his friend when he got MVP of the game.

your turn

Take this quiz and identify whether the statements are confident or cocky. Circle the description that applies.

1. You graciously accept a compliment.	Confident	Cocky
2. You brag to others and are always boasting.	Confident	Cocky
3. You admit you have weaknesses.	Confident	Cocky
4. You tell everyone your good grades even if they don't ask.	Confident	Cocky
5. You would never ask for help for fear that doing so would look bad.	Confident	Cocky
6. You are genuinely happy for others when they succeed.	Confident	Cocky
7. It frustrates you massively when others do better than you.	Confident	Cocky
8. You feel good about your accomplishments.	Confident	Cocky
9. You make excuses for your struggles.	Confident	Cocky
10. You put others down.	Confident	Cocky
11. You give genuine compliments to others.	Confident	Cocky
12. You cheer for your friends.	Confident	Cocky

Statements 2, 4, 5, 7, 9, and 10 reflect cockiness.

Statements 1, 3, 6, 8, 11, and 12 reflect confidence.

Do you know the difference between confident and cocky? How did you score?

Number of correct answers: _____

more practice

It's important to differentiate between confidence and cockiness. Confidence comes from believing in yourself and seeing your strengths and weaknesses in an accurate way. You feel good about your strengths so you don't need reassurance or putting other people down to define you. You also see your weaknesses accurately and work on them or use others as a resource so you don't let your weaknesses define you or get in your way. Cockiness comes from doubt, and because of this, you boast about artificially inflated abilities, compete with and criticize others to feel better about yourself, and make excuses for rather than working on your shortcomings. Practice some more with the quiz that follows. Read each story and circle the word that best describes each person's behavior.

1. SAT scores came out. John did better than he expected. He smiled inwardly and only revealed his good score to others when pressed.

   Confident   Cocky

2. The teacher passed back the biology test. Nick raised his hand and asked the class if anyone got a higher score than the 92 he received.

   Confident   Cocky

3. Zach's soccer team lost a close game. He sat on the sidelines, crying because he thought his team was better and that they should have won.

   Confident   Cocky

4. Carson's high-jump was an all-time personal record, but she still lost. Her personal success filled her with pride.

   Confident   Cocky

5. The play received bad reviews, so Mandy blamed the rest of the cast for bringing her performance down.

   Confident   Cocky

6. Emily's boyfriend went all-out when inviting her to the prom. She kept bragging and posting about how the proposal she received was better than everyone else's.

   Confident   Cocky

7. Sam rushed home to tell his parents the guidance department picked him to participate in a leadership conference.

   Confident   Cocky

8. Julie posts lots of pictures of friends, even if she isn't in them, rather than just sharing a bunch of selfies.

   Confident   Cocky

Answers:

Confident: 1, 4, 7, 8

Cocky: 2, 3, 5, 6

The Bottom Line: **Being confident is healthy while being cocky is problematic.**

Part 5

Confident Thinking

17 capture your thoughts

idea

Your history affects both your self-confidence and doubt. How you interpret situations in the moment influences how you feel and behave. Day-to-day well-being and success depend on your thinking. Simply put, situations don't cause you to feel a certain way. It's your perceptions and interpretations—your thinking—that influence how you feel, act, and physically respond. Don't make the mistake of underestimating the power of your thoughts. Thoughts have great influence and can cause you to unknowingly bolster false doubts instead of building accurate confidence.

Elijah

Elijah was getting ready for the big lacrosse tournament. He and his teammates were on the bus and totally pumped to go crush all of their opponents. The team knew they could dominate most of the other teams. As they were getting ready to start the first game, their coach let them know that several college scouts were watching to check them out. Elijah began thinking that maybe he wasn't good enough and had images of himself messing up. Self-doubt got in his way and he didn't have a very good game.

your turn

You can learn to pay attention to what you think. The first step in the process of examining your thinking is to capture your thoughts. What's going on in your head? It could be a thought. It could be an image, a mental picture of your thoughts. It could be the meaning you attach to that thought or image—or to a memory, the time of year, a dream, and so on. Read this narrative and practice capturing your thoughts.

It is lunchtime at school and the weather is exceptionally nice. Most people, including you, head outside to catch some rays. You hear two guys arguing and their voices are getting louder and louder.

What would you think? _____

_____

Did any of these thoughts come to mind? Check those that do:

_____ *This is getting interesting.*

_____ *I'm getting out of here before this turns into trouble.*

_____ *What a bunch of idiots.*

_____ *You can't trust anyone, I better watch my back.*

_____ *No one has any respect for anyone else.*

How would you feel? Circle all the descriptions that apply:

Anxious   Sad   Excited   Angry   Nervous   Uncomfortable   Neutral

What would you do? _____

_____

Would you do any of these things?

_____ Get closer to see the action.

_____ Disappear as quickly as you can.

_____ Stand your ground and stay right where you are.

Now the argument has gotten physical. The two guys are pushing and shoving each other.

What would you think? _____

_____

Do any of these thoughts come to mind? Check those that do:

_____ I've got to break this up.

_____ This is crazy, I'm out of here.

_____ Someone is going to get seriously hurt, I'll call for help.

How would you feel? Circle all the descriptions that apply:

Anxious   Sad   Excited   Angry   Nervous   Uncomfortable   Neutral

What would you do? _____

_____

Would you do any of these things?

_____ Get even closer to see the action.

_____ Disappear as quickly as you can.

_____ Jump in to help break it up.

Reflect on the ways what is going on around you directly influences how you feel and what you choose to do.

Let's imagine another situation. Try to capture your thoughts about it.

You are in math class and the teacher calls on one of your classmates. The classmate doesn't know the answer and is stumbling over her words. You don't know the answer either and the teacher is pressing this kid for an answer.

What would you think? _____

_____

Do any of these thoughts come to mind? Check those that do:

_____ *Please don't call on me.*

_____ *I'm in trouble if he finds out I don't know the answer, either.*

_____ *The teacher should move on and let someone who knows the answer talk.*

_____ *Clearly none of us know the answer—he should just tell us what it is.*

How would you feel? Circle any descriptions that apply:

Anxious   Sad   Excited   Angry   Nervous   Uncomfortable   Neutral

What would you do? _____

_____

Would you do any of these things?

_____ Shrink down in your seat and hope you're not noticed.

_____ Speak up to say that you don't know the answer, either. Ask the teacher to tell the class what it is.

_____ Ask another question to divert the teacher's attention.

_____ Ask to use the bathroom so there is no chance of being caught not knowing the answer.

The teacher is getting increasingly frustrated with the student. The teacher is turning red and his voice is getting louder. He starts to reprimand the student for being unprepared.

What would you think? _____

_____

Do any of these thoughts come to mind? Check those that do:

_____ *This is so unfair. The teacher should move on.*

_____ *I hope I'm not next.*

_____ *Who cares!*

What would you do? _____

_____

Would you do any of these things?

_____ Tense up and start to stress out.

_____ Tune the teacher out.

_____ Volunteer that, although you read the material, you are clueless as well.

Again, reflect on how what you think about the situation directly influences how you feel and choose to behave.

more practice

Over the next several days, when you notice yourself in an upsetting, unpleasant, or negative situation, ask yourself these questions.

What am I thinking?

How do I feel?

What will I do?

There's also a worksheet available for this exercise at http://www.newharbinger .com/34831, if you'd like to journal about your answers.

The Bottom Line: **Capture your thinking before your thoughts capture you.**

use your emotions as 18
warning lights

idea

When events are stressful, upsetting, unpredictable, or uncontrollable, you can get so overwhelmed by an emotion that your world is colored by it. The emotion might even cause you to handle things badly or act in a way that you later regret. By noticing your emotions and how intense they are in the moment, you put yourself back in the driver's seat and are able to decide how to proceed. When you recognize emotions as warning lights, you will keep them from overtaking your thinking. Being effective means choosing a course of action that maximizes the chance of a successful outcome.

Christy

Someone Christy doesn't know all that well said she thought Christy's boyfriend had cheated with someone from another school. Christy felt extremely angry and hurt. Her emotions were in the red zone. She wanted to hurt her boyfriend so she refused to give back the stuff he left at her house, ripped up all their pictures, and posted mean stories about him all over the Internet. Once she found out the rumor wasn't true, she tried to apologize but he wasn't interested in talking to her.

your turn

Here are some of the emotions that you may want to think about:

Angry	Frustrated	Mad
Annoyed	Guilty	Miserable
Anxious	Helpless	Overwhelmed
Ashamed	Hopeless	Panicked
Disappointed	Hurt	Rejected
Distressed	Insecure	Sad
Down	Irritated	Shy
Fearful	Lonely	Stressed

What are the emotions you experience most intensely?

_____

This exercise will help you think about an emotion as the warning light that signals you to pay attention to your thoughts.

On the scale below, a 0 means you're not experiencing the emotion at all and 10 means you're experiencing the emotion to its fullest. When you are at an 8 or higher, typically that means the emotion is taking over, which results in a distorted view of the world. A 6 or 7 means that while you may have some objectivity, your feelings can still lead to a skewed viewpoint.

0----------1----------2----------3----------4----------5----------6----------7----------8----------9----------10

Think about the last time your emotions got the better of you.

What was the situation? _____

_____

What was the main emotion you experienced and, using the intensity scale, how high did it get?

_____

_____

more practice

When your emotions are running too high, you can get caught up in thoughts that rev your feelings even higher. This is what it means to be reactive. Here are some examples of thoughts you might have when your emotions are overheated.

I feel bad so the situation is bad.	I feel bad and can't deal so I won't.
I feel bad so the situation will turn out badly.	I feel bad so something bad will happen.
I feel bad so something bad did happen.	My feelings are right.
They made me feel bad so I'll make them feel bad.	I have to do something to stop feeling bad.
I felt this bad in the past and it was a bad situation.	I have to listen to my feelings.

Next time your feelings are running high, pay attention so that you can capture your thoughts. Then notice how they play a role in the action you take. Use the following format any time you want to make note of the situation, your feelings, and how you act as a result.

Situation: _____

_____

Feelings (circle all that apply):

Angry	Guilty	Overwhelmed
Annoyed	Helpless	Panicked
Anxious	Hopeless	Rejected
Ashamed	Hurt	Sad
Disappointed	Insecure	Shy
Distressed	Irritated	Stressed
Down	Lonely	Other:
Fearful	Mad	_____
Frustrated	Miserable	_____

Thoughts: _____

_____

_____

Actions: _____

_____

_____

The Bottom Line: **Strong emotions are more likely to make you reactive than effective.**

19 use your body to pay attention to your thinking

idea

You might be more aware of shifts in your body than variations in your thoughts—especially in stressful or challenging situations. When you notice physical changes in your body, it can be a sign that it's time to capture your thoughts and check out what you're thinking. By following this strategy, you may find yourself making better choices.

Lisa

Lisa was about to stand in front of her English class and give a presentation. Her mouth was dry and it felt hard to talk. Her body was shaking, her heart was beating out of her chest, and she was having a hard time breathing. *I'm freaking out,* she thought, *I might literally pass out. I'd never live it down if I stood up and passed out right in front of the class.*

your turn

Here are some of the body responses you might experience when you're in the grip of a negative emotion:

Achey	Dizziness	Racing Mind	Tapping fingers
Backache	Headache	Restlessness	Tense shoulders
Breathless	Jitteriness	Shaking	Tension
Butterflies	Nausea	Shaking feet	Tight chest
Chest pain	Needing to urinate or defecate	Shortness of breath	Tight muscles
Clammy hands		Sick	Trembling
Crying	Pounding heart	Sweating	Upset stomach

What are the main body responses you tend to experience when you are sad, disappointed, or hurt?

_____

_____

What are the main body responses you tend to experience when you are scared, anxious, or fearful?

_____

_____

What are the main body responses you tend to experience when you are annoyed, angry, or frustrated?

_____

_____

more practice

You can become aware of which body responses pair with specific emotions. Use sensation as an opportunity to ask yourself what you are thinking and try to capture your thoughts. Notice if your thoughts influence the action you take.

Here are some examples of what you might think when your body is reacting:

- I'm having a heart attack.

- I'm losing control.

- I'm going crazy.

- I can't breathe.

- I'll throw up right here.

- My thoughts won't stop racing.

- I won't make it to the bathroom.

- My voice is totally shaking.

- I can't stand it.

- This will never stop.

- My head will explode.

- My hands won't stop shaking.

- This is getting worse.

- I have no control.

- It's always going to happen this way.

- I have to make it stop.

- What will people think?

- This is a disaster.

Think about the last time your body symptoms felt intense and got the better of you. What was the situation?

_____

_____

What were the main bodily reactions you experienced?

_____

_____

What did you think?

_____

_____

What did you do?

_____

_____

_____

The Bottom Line: **Use your bodily sensations to capture your thoughts so you can choose how to act.**

20 chill-out strategies

idea

It is possible to stay in control even when you feel out of control. The key is not letting you freak yourself out. Strong emotions and bodily sensations can affect your thinking and what actions you take—but you have the power to chill yourself out.

Jared

Jared was angry when his parents grounded him for getting home an hour late. He thought that it wasn't fair and he wanted them to hear his side of the story. He kept yelling louder so that they might actually hear him. He got so mad that he threw his phone and broke it. Later, he realized that all his reaction did was cut his lifeline to his friends, double his punishment, and stop his parents from listening to him. Jared thought, *If I could hit the rewind button, I'd realize the punishment was fair, own my part, and be cool with it.*

your turn

Think back to the last time your emotions were over the top, to the point that you could feel it in your body. Imagine yourself back in that situation and using some of these chill-out strategies.

- Breathe in slowly through your nose and breathe out slowly through your mouth.

- Listen to calming music.

- Sing your favorite song and focus on the words.

- Go for a run or take a walk.

- Call a friend or family member.

- Watch a TV show or movie that makes you happy.

- Find a comedy bit on the Internet and laugh.

- Think through the good stuff that happened that day or the day before.

- Do some stretching.

- Let go of mental tension by relaxing your muscles.

- Plan a fabulous vacation in your mind.

- Get busy doing something for a set amount of time and give your brain a break.

- Read a book or magazine.

- Schedule a predetermined amount of time to play a video or computer game.

- Do something creative.

- Plan a meal or check out menus.

Example:

Emma couldn't find her hockey stick and was convinced her sister took it and lost it. Instead of storming into her sister's room and laying into her for losing the hockey stick, she went for a run and then calmly checked out her suspicion.

Try the following scenario. What chill-out strategy might you use? You check your grades online and see two of your completed assignments are missing and graded as zeros. Instead of letting your emotions get the best of you, first you _____ and only then do you e-mail your teacher.

Think of the last time you would have benefited from a chill-out strategy. What did you do and what could you have tried?

Situation: _____

_____

What you did: _____

_____

What chill-out strategy you could have tried instead: _____

_____

_____

more practice

Like any skill or talent, the more you apply these strategies, the better. Pick a few of chill-out strategies from the list that appeal to you. Next time you have an emotional moment, try one or several of them, see how easy or difficult it is to chill out and whether it helps you behave more confidently.

Situation: _____

_____

Chill-out strategy tried: _____

_____

_____

Did you feel more in control? Circle one answer: YES   NO

The Bottom Line: **I'm more in control when I am chill.**

21 gather the facts

idea

Examining your thoughts puts you in charge of how you feel, how your body responds, and how you choose to act. Once you've chilled yourself out, it's time to check out your thinking. The first step is capturing your thoughts. Then, once you have identified them, check those thoughts for accuracy. Thoughts can be distorted and not a reflection of the truth. When this happens, an inaccurate viewpoint is guiding you instead of reality. It's time to start thinking about your thinking and to practice this skill as you would any other. Gathering the facts is one way to investigate the accuracy of your thinking and regain control.

Sam

Sam walked into class and everyone looked at him. They were all laughing hysterically. He automatically thought that everyone was laughing at him. Feeling uncomfortable, he took his seat and didn't talk to anyone. Had Sam gathered the facts, he would have found out that Joe had just told a joke.

your turn

A great motto to remember is: "Just because you think it or feel it doesn't mean it's true." That's why it's important to gather evidence for, and also against, the thought you have captured. To do this, rather than going with your personal interpretation pretend you are a scientist collecting objective observations.

Here's an exercise that will help you practice.

Think of a recent situation that upset you. Capture the thoughts you had and list them here.

_____

_____

_____

_____

_____

For each captured thought, write out the facts that support or don't support it.

Captured thought: _____

Facts That Support This Thought	Facts That Don't Support This Thought

Captured thought: _____

Facts That Support This Thought	Facts That Don't Support This Thought

Captured thought: _____

Facts That Support This Thought	Facts That Don't Support This Thought

What do you conclude from the facts you collected? Was the original thought true? Exaggerated? Biased? Unhelpful? Do the facts lead you to a new perspective on the situation? If so, record it in the space below.

_____

_____

_____

If you want to try this experiment again, you can download a worksheet version of this exercise at http://www.newharbinger.com/34831.

more practice

Over the course of the next several days, use the shifts you notice in your moods or body sensations to remind you to capture your thoughts and question how true they are. Note the situation, your mood, and body sensations below, then use the table for your thoughts.

Activating situation: _____

_____

Mood: _____

_____

Body sensations: _____

_____

_____

Activating situation: _____

_____

Mood: _____

_____

Body sensations: _____

_____

_____

Captured Thought	Facts That Support Thought	Facts That Don't Support Thought	How True Was The Thought?

How do you feel now that you've looked at the facts?

_____

_____

_____

When you are on the go, you can recreate this table in a notebook or even on a napkin. (You can also download a worksheet version of the exercise at the book's website: http://www.newharbinger.com/34831.)

The Bottom Line: **If you remember that your thinking affects your emotions, body responses, and actions, you can regain control.**

22 examine all possible options

idea

The way you think about something may not be the only viewpoint and it probably isn't absolute truth. Just going with your immediate thought can land you in hot water because you're running with the inaccurate, unassessed, not checked-out thought. This can significantly affect how you handle any given situation. A better strategy than following a snap judgment is to open your mind to consider all possible options.

Ben

The math teacher called Ben into her office to discuss the D on his test. Ben's muscles tensed, his heart started to race and he automatically thought that the teacher was going to tell him that she and his guidance counselor had decided he would be better off in the lower-level math class. As a result, Ben walked into her office on the defensive, demanding that she give him another chance rather than force him into a less advanced class. The teacher looked at him, baffled, and replied that she only wanted to review his mistakes with him. But after his verbal tirade, she was feeling taken aback.

your turn

Over the course of the next several days, pay attention to when you notice a shift in your mood or body, record it, and then write down each captured thought on a separate line. Then, to broaden your sense of all the possible interpretations and viewpoints, complete this exercise. Use the downloadable worksheet available at http://www.newharbinger.com/34831 if you need to.

Write out a recent situation that upset you:

_____

_____

What feelings or body sensations did you notice? Make note of them here:

_____

_____

Next, write out your captured thoughts:

_____

_____

_____

Now, respond to these questions in the space provided:

- If you were a fly on the wall, what would your understanding of the situation be?

_____

_____

- Pick a family member who you think typically has a good point of view on things. What do you think that person would say?

  _____

  _____

- If someone you cared about was in the exact same situation, what would you say to that person?

  _____

  _____

- What are some other possible explanations for what happened?

  _____

  _____

- If you could transport yourself a day into the future, what would you think about the situation?

  _____

  _____

- If you could transport yourself many years into the future, what might you think about the situation?

  _____

  _____

Write out the new perspective you have gained:

_____

_____

_____

more practice

Think about another current upsetting situation and once again list those upsetting thoughts.

Write out a recent situation that upset you:

_____

_____

What feelings or body sensations did you notice? Make note of them here:

_____

_____

Next, write out your captured thoughts:

_____

_____

_____

Now, respond to these questions in the space provided:

- If you were a fly on the wall, what would your understanding of the situation be?

_____

_____

- Pick a family member who you think typically has a good point of view on things. What do you think that person would say?

  _____

  _____

- If someone you cared about was in the exact same situation, what would you say to that person?

  _____

  _____

- What are some other possible explanations for what happened?

  _____

  _____

- If you could transport yourself a day into the future, what would you think about the situation?

  _____

  _____

- If you could transport yourself many years into the future, what might you think about the situation?

  _____

  _____

Write out the new perspective you have gained:

_____

_____

_____

Were your original thoughts about the situation untrue or even partially untrue?

Circle one answer: YES NO

Is your original view of the situation still valid?

Circle one answer: YES NO

Have you gained a new perspective?

Circle one answer: YES NO

The next time your thoughts upset you, try looking at the evidence and seeing the situation from different perspectives. Remember the new perspectives you have gained through this exercise and use them in the future.

The Bottom Line: **It's helpful to check out your thinking
by looking at it from as many angles as possible.**

23 consider alternative viewpoints

idea

When faced with an unresolved or confusing situation, it is natural for your mind to jump to the first negative, worst-case conclusion that pops into your head. But this viewpoint may be wrong and can cause you a lot of unnecessary upset. Instead, you can get into the habit of considering all the possibilities as you wait for facts to come in.

Alison

Every time Alison calls Tori, she always answers with "I can't talk, I'll call you back." Alison's first reaction is to think, *She always does this to me. I'm the only one she treats this way. She must find it a burden to talk to me.* The truth is that Tori treats everyone this way because she is overcommitted and pulled in too many directions. This makes it difficult for her to find the time to talk to anyone.

your turn

Get into the habit of seeing all the possible alternative viewpoints when faced with a confusing or unresolved situation. Read the situations below and see what kind of thoughts jump into your head.

Situation: You have just sent a text to your friend Dan and there is no response.

Check any of the following viewpoints that you jump to:

_____ He must be busy; he'll text me when he can.

_____ His phone is probably dead.

_____ He's stuck somewhere with no cell service.

_____ He is unable to text right now.

_____ He is purposely avoiding me.

_____ He is probably still mad at me.

_____ He is trying to leave me out of the plans for tonight.

Situation: You are leaving town tomorrow. Your friends said they would drop by around seven o'clock and it's now nine o'clock.

Check any of the following viewpoints you jump to:

_____ No worries, they will be here eventually.

_____ Whatever time this crowd says, it always means hours later.

_____ They're still coming because someone would have let me know if plans had changed.

_____ It's possible something interfered with their plans.

_____ They're not coming.

_____ I guess they're not as good of friends as I thought.

_____ Typical of them to blow me off again.

Situation: You just gave a presentation in class.

Check any of the following viewpoints you jump to:

_____ I nailed this.

_____ I really knew my stuff and everyone could tell.

_____ I'm not sure what the students thought, but my teacher seemed to be pleased.

_____ I'm sure I did fine.

_____ I know I didn't flunk, but I'm not sure how well I did.

_____ I blew it.

_____ Everyone could tell how uncomfortable I was and I'm sure it's going to affect my grade.

Situation: You just took a difficult exam.

Check any of the following viewpoints you jump to:

_____ I can't believe how well I did.

_____ I'm sure I did the same as the majority of the class.

_____ That was really tough, but I'm sure I did just fine.

_____ I hope I did okay, but who knows?

_____ I definitely bombed the test.

_____ I bet everyone did poorly, but I'm sure I did the worst.

_____ There goes my GPA.

Were you inclined to check the last three viewpoints for each scenario? If so, you are building the negative habit of looking for the worst outcome, even before you get the facts. If you more often checked the first three viewpoints in each list, then you have a more balanced, positive viewpoint and you are on track to building helpful habits that support self-confidence.

more practice

When faced with an uncertain outcome, you can build a new habit of thinking that supports confidence by seeing all possible alternative viewpoints. Here are four situations with uncertain outcomes. List as many realistic perceptions or viewpoints as you can in the space provided. For reference, you can use the first three items on each checklist in the previous exercise and revise any that seem similar to the last three viewpoints.

Situation: You have not heard back about a job you applied for.

Viewpoints: _____

_____

_____

_____

Situation: All of your friends received invites to the post-prom party, but you didn't.

Viewpoints: _____

_____

_____

_____

Situation: You spent hours on an English paper and have been waiting more than a week for your grade.

Viewpoints: _____

_____

_____

_____

Situation: You show up for a party and it looks like no one is there.

Viewpoints: _____

_____

_____

_____

Now use a situation from your life and come up with as many possible viewpoints as you can.

Your Situation: _____

Viewpoints: _____

_____

_____

_____

The Bottom Line: **Don't let your negative first conclusion get the best of you when there are many viewpoints to consider.**

24 try not to jump to conclusions or overgeneralize

idea

It's tempting to take one fact or detail from a situation and, in your mind, run with your interpretation. But you're not considering all the information. It's like watching a few minutes of a movie or reading one page of a book and deciding you hate the story or a character. You don't have enough information to form a reasonable or valid opinion and have instead formed a snap conclusion or overgeneralization.

Melissa

When Melissa's friends don't text her back right away, she makes snap conclusions: they are blowing her off, don't want her along, or are purposely avoiding her. The truth could be that they didn't see her text, their phone was dead, they were driving, or they just haven't had time to respond.

Similarly, when Melissa's grade on a paper wasn't posted right away, she thought her teacher never got her paper and didn't even consider that it just hadn't been scored yet.

Melissa's coach is usually friendly, but one day he walked by without saying hello. Melissa's snap conclusion was that he was either mad at her or unhappy with something she did, or that he didn't like her anymore. But he simply didn't see her because he was preoccupied with the class he was about to teach.

your turn

Here are some good strategies to use that will prevent you from jumping to conclusions before you have all the facts.

- Don't make predictions about a situation before it actually happens.

- Take the magnifying glass off the one piece of information you keep thinking about.

- Avoid focusing on the one element that upset you, while leaving out other facts and details.

- To see the situation clearly, give each fact and detail equal importance.

- Collect as many facts as possible.

- Before jumping to a conclusion, remind yourself to wait until the situation has played out all the way.

- Base an accurate conclusion on the bigger picture and not just one piece of information.

more practice

Think of a situation in which you snapped to a conclusion without looking at all the possibilities and answer these questions in the space provided.

What happened? _____

_____

_____

When you capture your thoughts, what snap conclusion did you jump to?

_____

_____

_____

What are some possible alternative conclusions?

_____

_____

_____

Because time has passed since this situation happened, how was your snap conclusion different from the truth that eventually became clear to you?

_____

_____

_____

even more practice

Run an experiment this week: when you capture a snap conclusion that is causing you distress, try using the strategies previously offered in this activity. Then write down how these strategies helped you. (If you need more space for this—or if you want your experiment to run a few weeks longer—you can download a worksheet for this exercise from http://www.newharbinger.com/34831.)

When you captured your thoughts, what snap conclusion did you jump to?

_____

_____

_____

What strategies can help you see more possible conclusions?

_____

_____

_____

What are some possible alternative conclusions?

_____

_____

_____

Did you find using these strategies helpful? If yes, how were they helpful?

_____

_____

_____

Which conclusion reflected the truth, the snap conclusion or one of the alternatives you considered?

_____

_____

_____

The Bottom Line: **Stop and think. Rather than making a snap judgment, take the time to consider all the information.**

Part 6

Confident Actions

25 how doubt gets in your way

idea

Doubt-driven thinking is the direct result of doubt. It causes you to distort your observations of external situations and internal experiences in a negative way. Doubt-driven thinking is directly connected to your doubt label. The doubt label is the negative name you call yourself when you are experiencing uncertainty, insecurity, self-criticism, distress, upset, or vulnerability. When doubt shapes your viewpoint, you act in ways you may not otherwise choose. These actions can lead to negative consequences or take you in a direction that opposes your values or goals. Doubt-driven actions are ineffective strategies. Here are some typical ineffective strategies that are caused by doubt:

Avoidance

- Avoiding

- Quitting

- Distracting

Perfectionism

- Seeking perfection

- Controlling

- Pleasing

- Worrying

Ineffective Communication

- Being passive

- Manipulating

- Defending

Jack

Jack has had his driver's permit for so long that, if he doesn't take the test soon, he will have to start the process all over again. He knows having his driver's license will come in handy and that without it his mobility is limited. But he can't seem to schedule the test because he fears he will flunk it. And given how uncomfortable driving feels to him, Jack even questions whether he wants to drive at all.

your turn

In these examples, take note of the ways doubt can lead to ineffective strategies.

Example 1: You are thinking about applying for a college that would be a reach for you to get into.

Your doubt-driven thoughts might say:

- *I have no chance.*

- *Completing the application would just be a waste of time.*

- *People will think I am stupid for bothering.*

What might you think?

_____

_____

_____

Doubt-driven thinking might lead you to:

- Never complete the application

- Halfheartedly complete the application

- Apply only for the schools you are likely to get into

What might you do?

_____

_____

_____

Recognize that these are ineffective, doubt-driven avoidance strategies that minimize the chance of being accepted or even guarantee no acceptance.

Imagine that your doubt-driven thinking labeled you a failure and told you that you weren't good enough. How might you use this situation to confirm that your doubts are true?

_____

_____

What other doubt labels might be confirmed? Some examples include: incompetent, incapable, undesirable, stupid, inadequate, airheaded, bad, helpless, or absentminded.

_____   _____   _____

Which of your personal doubt labels might be activated by this situation?

_____   _____   _____

Example 2: You would like to try out for something, whether a sports team, chorale, orchestra, or band.

Your doubt-driven thoughts might say:

- *I'm not good enough.*

- *I don't have a chance.*

- *It's too much effort, why bother?*

What might you think?

_____

_____

_____

Doubt-driven thinking might lead you to:

- Avoid the tryout

- Halfheartedly give it a shot

- Show up late, leave early, or miss some of the tryouts

What might you do?

_____

_____

_____

Recognize that these are ineffective, doubt-driven avoidance strategies that minimize the chance of being chosen or even guarantee that you won't make the cut.

Imagine that your doubt-driven thinking has labeled you a failure, an outcast, or has determined that you are undesirable. How might you use this situation to confirm that your doubts are true?

_____

_____

What other doubt labels might be confirmed? Some examples include: worthless, incapable, bad, average, incompetent, a loser, or lazy.

Which of your personal doubt labels might be activated by this situation?

_____   _____   _____

Example 3: You are preparing to write a paper that will count for a large part of your grade.

Your doubt-driven thoughts might say:

- *My grade depends on this paper, so it has to be perfect.*

- *The paper will never come out the way I want it to, so why bother trying?*

- *This is too much effort, I can't do it.*

What might you think?

_____

_____

_____

Doubt-driven thinking might lead you to:

- Keep trying to make your paper perfect, even though you will miss the due date

- Avoid the situation completely and never start the paper

- Start the paper, but let distractions take you off task

What might you do?

_____

_____

_____

Recognize that both avoidance and perfectionism are ineffective, doubt-driven strategies that can cause you to procrastinate, miss deadlines, or never find satisfaction with the work you produce.

Imagine that your doubt-driven thinking labeled you a failure or told you that you were incompetent. How might you use this situation to confirm your doubts?

_____

_____

What other doubt labels might be confirmed? Some examples include: I'm helpless, weak, worthless, useless, inferior, incompetent, incapable, absentminded, airheaded.

Which of your personal doubt labels might get activated by this situation?

_____   _____   _____

Example 4: You would like to ask one of your classmates to a school dance.

Your doubt-driven thoughts might say:

- *I will probably be turned down.*

- *I will look like a fool.*

- *I'm not very much fun. No one is going to want to hang out with me at the dance.*

What might you think?

_____

_____

_____

Doubt-driven thinking might lead you to:

- Avoid asking

- Get someone else to ask the classmate for you

- Skip the event completely

What might you do?

_____

_____

_____

Recognize that, by using these ineffective, doubt-driven strategies of avoidance and poor communication, you would miss out on something fun and you would not get to hang out with the person you wanted to go with.

Imagine that your doubt-driven thinking labeled you unworthy, unlikable, and undesirable. How might you use this situation to confirm your doubt?

_____

_____

What other doubt labels might be confirmed? Some examples include: weird, uncool, awkward, average, unattractive, odd, or lazy. You might also tell yourself you don't measure up.

Which of your personal doubt labels might get activated by this situation?

_____   _____   _____

more practice

When doubt seems to be in charge, become aware of the ineffective action strategies that result.

Think back to a time when you avoided something, tried to be perfect, or didn't effectively communicate.

What was the situation?

_____

_____

What were your doubt-driven thoughts?

_____

_____

What ineffective action did you take?

_____

_____

_____

Did you use doubt-driven thinking to label yourself? What was the name you called yourself?

_____

The Bottom Line: **Beware of letting doubt guide your behavior.**

133

26 stop avoiding

idea

Everyone has behavioral strategies that he or she uses to minimize stress and make life easier. Sometimes those behaviors work, but more often these strategies don't work, and may even make things worse. There are three major types of ineffective behaviors: avoidance, perfectionism, and ineffective communication.

While all of these behaviors are pervasive problems that keep you from achieving your goals and compromise your well-being, avoidance is the most harmful. Typically driven by insecurity and fear, avoidance stops you from dealing directly with things that are important. When you don't face a task, you can create bigger problems, leave important work unfinished, and miss opportunities. You put yourself at greater risk for punishments and penalties, and you miss out on the positive accomplishments necessary to build confidence.

Lynn

The theater department posted a sign-up sheet for auditions for a play the following Monday. Lynn had dreamed of a role in a high school play, but thought she would never get a good part. So she stood in front of the sign-up sheet, trying to decide whether to sign up. Wanting to think about it further, she walked away. Days flew by and she was still thinking about it. But then, in her inability to make a decision, she missed the deadline. She then realized the decision had been made for her.

your turn

There are three kinds of avoidance strategies: evading, quitting, and distracting. When faced with a difficult situation, which of these do you use? Check all that apply.

_____ You evade everything by dodging things. You sidestep problems and avoid doing the tasks that might resolve them.

_____ You quit or give up before trying much, refusing to see things through to the end.

_____ You distract your attention from the priority task and get busy doing something else, such as watching television, playing video games, or using alcohol or drugs.

When was the last time you had a goal and evaded, quit, or distracted yourself before reaching it?

_____

Was that strategy a good choice? Why or why not?

_____

_____

What impact did this choice have on your self-confidence?

_____

_____

more practice

The next time a difficult situation comes up, think about using the following strategy to help you replace avoidance with effective action. The avoidance habit is hard to break because it feels protective, as it helps you avoid facing difficult or unpleasant situations. But then you'll never achieve your goals or resolve your problems. So instead, when avoidance is getting in your way, choose the behaviors that work best in each situation.

Here is a list of effective action options. Mark all actions you already do and all that you would consider trying.

Effective Action Option	Do Already	Would Try
Solve the Problem: Define the problem. Consider your options. Weigh the pros and cons. Pick a solution.		
Prioritize: Stay focused so that distractions don't get in the way of taking care of urgent tasks.		
Stop Delay Tactics: Refuse to believe excuses and give in to distractions. Keep on task.		
Schedule Timed Breaks: Prevent impulsive interruptions for snacks or drinks by planning your break times.		
Take Action: Make a plan and write it on your schedule. Tackle the task head-on because action can happen even if you don't feel like doing it or don't want to do it. Start doing.		
Just Try: Give the task your best effort and make an attempt.		
Keep It Simple: Be clear about what the task is and don't make it more complicated than that.		

Effective Action Option	Do Already	Would Try
Use Help: First try the task on your own, but if you need additional information or assistance use your resources.		
Small Steps: Break the task down into smaller, manageable pieces so you aren't trying to start and finish a big task all at once.		
Each Accomplishment Deserves Credit: Write down each thing you accomplish so you can appreciate how much you have done.		
Be Okay Not Knowing the Results: Dive in and do it anyway, so that anxiety and fear of the unknown don't stop you before you even begin.		
Stay Focused and Present: Stay on task and focus all of your attention. It's not the time to check Facebook, Instagram, or Snapchat, text friends, or glance at the TV.		
Follow Through: Hang in there and see the task through until it's done.		

even more practice

Think about a situation in which you chose an avoidance strategy.

Describe the situation: _____

_____

How did you avoid it?

_____

_____

What impact did doing that have on your self-confidence?

_____

_____

What effective action strategy, or strategies, could you use next time?

_____

_____

How might this new option affect your self-confidence?

_____

_____

The Bottom Line: **Don't let avoidance block your success.**

cut out strategies that
don't work

idea

Your self-confidence grows when you stop using strategies that don't work and take effective action. Perfectionism, control, pleasing others, and worry work against you. You won't feel good enough when you can't live up to unreasonable standards. You will feel overwhelmed by pressure when you demand complete control. You will miss out on getting your needs met because you are too busy pleasing others. And you won't achieve your goals because you're so busy worrying, you can't address the problem. When you learn to replace the strategies that don't work with more effective action options, you will grow your self-confidence.

Nicole

Nicole wakes up and immediately stresses over what to wear. She believes that if she doesn't pick the perfect outfit, she won't fit in with her friends. She obsesses over whether to wear her hair down or put it up, thinking it is a determining factor in how people view her. When she arrived at school this morning, her friend asked what she thought of the concert last night. Nicole froze up, thinking she had to give the right answer. Meanwhile, her friend wondered why Nicole was being so standoffish and unfriendly.

your turn

When faced with a difficult situation, which ineffective strategies do you use? Check all that apply:

_____ **Seeking Perfectionism:** You hold yourself to an ideal standard. Everything must be just right. You set goals that can't be realistically defined or achieved.

_____ **Controlling:** You want total control and have to be in charge of everyone and everything. You insist on doing things your way and getting what you want. You wish you could be in more than one place at a time.

_____ **Pleasing:** You are concerned with pleasing others. You often lose sight of your own needs in the process of making others happy. You have a hard time saying no.

_____ **Worrying:** You worry about things that have already happened and things that might happen. You have nagging thoughts that focus on "what if" and dwell on the worst that could happen.

When was the last time you didn't achieve a goal because you sought perfection, took complete control, pleased others, or worried?

_____

_____

Was that strategy a good choice? Why or why not?

_____

_____

How did this strategy affect your self-confidence?

_____

_____

_____

more practice

You can change up your strategies and apply more effective action while at the same time accepting that you're going to fall short in some way, at some point. This is not because you're not good enough; it's because you are human, with a unique set of strengths and weaknesses. Accept that it is impossible to get everything exactly right all the time. If you let go of perfection, your work will not become second rate; you won't settle, slack off, or become lazy, and people will not see you as selfish. There are more effective strategies than perfectionism, and the following is a list of effective action options to use when perfectionism is getting in your way. Mark which actions you do already and which ones you would try.

Effective Action Option	Do Already	Would Try
Develop Realistic Standards: Accept that in many situations, good enough is really good enough.		
Make a Choice: Use the information you have to make a reasonable decision and accept that there is no perfect decision.		
Yield: Take control some of the time, but not all of the time.		
Take a Team Approach: Let others participate and share the responsibility.		
Give Up the Need to Always Please Others: Make your needs and feelings part of the equation.		
Be Logical: Don't take care of others at the expense of your own well-being.		
Turn Off Your Worry: Focus on the facts and know that worry doesn't keep you safe, change the outcome, or help you solve the problem.		
Stay in the Present: Think in terms of "for now" and not "forever."		

even more practice

Think about a situation in which you chose an ineffective strategy.

Describe the situation: _____

_____

Which ineffective strategy did you use?

_____

_____

What impact did that strategy have on your self-confidence?

_____

_____

Which alternative strategies from the list could you use next time?

_____

_____

How might the new effective action option affect your self-confidence?

_____

_____

_____

Bottom Line: **Turn off perfectionism, the need for control, the need to please others, and useless worry.**

28 communicate your point

idea

Ineffective communication happens when you have not clearly expressed your message. You fail to let others know that something was a problem for you, you were unable to share how you felt about it, or you weren't able to express what you want instead. Failing to get your point across can lead to misunderstandings, and the people involved might feel unappreciated, undervalued, overworked, dumped on, taken advantage of, or not considered. When you don't communicate well, you miss opportunities, compromise yourself, and hurt your self-esteem. If you can learn to replace ineffective communication with effective communication, you will achieve more of your goals and improve your self-confidence.

Mattheus

Mattheus was supposed to intern for a family friend during the summer. He had received an e-mail saying that someone from the company would be in touch, but summer was approaching and no one had contacted him. He called the office, but when no one answered, he hung up without leaving a message. When he sat down to write the company an e-mail, he didn't know what to say so he gave up. Days passed, then weeks. Summer started and Mattheus still passively waited to hear from the company, a strategy that could ruin his opportunity for a summer internship.

your turn

When faced with a difficult situation, which ineffective communication strategies do you use? Check all that apply:

_____ **Being Passive:** You are unassertive and hold back rather than speaking or acting directly. You fail to clearly express what you want, feel, or need.

_____ **Manipulating:** You get others to do what you want by twisting the facts or maneuvering in a way that serves your best interest. You might present partial information, omit facts and details, exaggerate insignificant details, hedge bets, pile on facts to support one side, or purposely leave some people uninformed.

_____ **Defending:** You often feel attacked, so you make excuses or attack back. You tend to stop listening and start reacting.

When was the last time you used ineffective communication and it kept you from your goals?

_____

Was that strategy a good choice? Why or why not?

_____

_____

What impact did the choice have on your self-confidence?

_____

_____

_____

more practice

Instead of communicating ineffectively, take effective action by communicating clearly and saying directly what you think, feel, need, or want. Doing this means taking a stand for what is right for you. Don't let others persuade you to do things that may put you at risk, compromise your needs, or hurt others. Instead of getting stuck in the communication style that you feel comfortable with, try replacing it with what works.

The following is a list of effective action options to use when ineffective communication is getting in your way. Mark which actions you do already and which ones you would try.

Effective Action Option	Do Already	Would Try
State the Facts: Be willing to tell people what they did or said that bothered you.		
Speak Up: Ask for what you want. Be clear, be specific, and let others know what you want to do.		
Listen to Others: Acknowledging what others think, feel, or want makes them more willing to compromise.		
Compromise: Find a solution that works best for you *and* includes the needs of the people you care about. Be willing to be flexible.		
Be Assertive: Express yourself clearly and mean what you say.		
Present the Full Picture: Be accurate and straightforward.		
Give the Appropriate Weight to Information: Don't exaggerate to make a point, and don't minimize how important something is to you.		

Effective Action Option	Do Already	Would Try
Try to See Both Sides: The truth is usually a mixture of your view and someone else's view of a situation.		
Take Responsibility: Instead of making excuses, acknowledge your role.		
Be Objective: Consider the facts before you react.		
Don't Blow Up: Keep your cool so you can effectively deliver your message.		

Think about a situation in which you chose an ineffective communication strategy.

Describe the situation: _____

_____

How did you use ineffective communication?

_____

_____

What impact did that have on your self-confidence?

_____

_____

_____

Which alternative strategies from the list could you use next time?

_____

_____

_____

How might the new effective action option affect your self-confidence?

_____

_____

_____

The Bottom Line: **Speak up, and be willing to listen and compromise.**

Part 7

Confident Under Pressure

29 do away with perfectionism

idea

Defining "perfect" is impossible, since there is no such thing as perfection. Whether something is perfect depends on your point of view. Perfectionism forces you to always have to be the best, rather than to work at your personal, realistic best. Perfectionists hold themselves to unrealistically high standards for everything they care about. Logically, it's impossible to be perfect in all situations, all the time. Emotionally, perfectionists struggle to believe that, so they are critical of themselves and others.

Andy, Callie, and Jason

Andy gets his English test back and sees a score of 92 at the top. Immediately, he raises his hand and asks, "Did anyone in the class get a grade higher than 92?" Even though no one answers, internally Andy beats himself up for not doing better.

Callie is doing her floor routine during the gymnastics competition. But she can't enjoy being in the moment, doing what she loves. She is too busy focusing on each tiny detail of her routine, internally taking off points for every microscopic misstep.

Jason is doing a group project for his business class and doesn't allow anyone else in his group to do any of the work. He worries that they will make a mistake and it will cost him an A grade.

your turn

Do an Internet search for the names of several famous people you admire. Write down their strengths and successes, as well as their weaknesses, flaws, and failings.

Example: _Michael Jordan_

Things You Admire About This Person	Things You See As Weaknesses Or Flaws
Led the Chicago Bulls to six NBA championships	Tried out for the varsity basketball team his sophomore year and didn't make the cut
Won MVP five times	Missed baskets
One of the best basketball players ever	Lost many games
Donates to charity	Had gambling difficulties
Involved in business	Divorced his first wife

Person 1: _____

Things You Admire About This Person	Things You See As Weaknesses Or Flaws

Person 2: _____

Things You Admire About This Person	Things You See As Weaknesses Or Flaws

Look at all the tables you filled in with descriptions of famous people. Consider what you wrote in the columns on the right-hand side. What does this say about each person's perfection?

Example: Michael Jordan excelled in many areas of his life, but he also made plenty of mistakes and lost many games. But rather than beating himself up and getting in his own way, he loved competing and pushed himself to always perform better.

What can you say about the perfection of the people you chose to research?

_____

_____

Does the information on the right-hand side of the tables completely change the amount of respect and admiration you have for these people?

Circle one answer: YES   NO

Can you see them as humans who have both strengths and weaknesses, who have experienced successes as well as difficulties?

Circle one answer: YES   NO

Do you have more respect and admiration for them now that you can see them this way?

Circle one answer: YES   NO

more practice

During the next week, intentionally make one minor mistake each day. Use the chart to record your initial prediction (what you think will happen) and then record the actual outcome (what did happen). For example, on Monday Joe pretended he had forgotten a new friend's name. He said to her, "I've forgotten your name, can you tell it to me again? She responded, "It's Meghan. No worries, I do that all the time." On Tuesday, Joe left a typo in the e-mail he sent to a friend about a group project. On Wednesday, Joe purposefully gave a cashier the wrong amount of money and when she let him know he overpaid, he kindly thanked her for correcting him. On Thursday, as the team was about to head to the field Joe grabbed his friend's jersey rather than his own. On Friday, he texted a friend to say he was running ten minutes late because he lost track of time.

	Prediction (What You Think Will Happen)	Outcome (What Did Happen)
Monday		
Tuesday		
Wednesday		
Thursday		
Friday		
Saturday		
Sunday		

Based on your experiences this week, what conclusions can you make about how your predictions compare with the actual outcomes?

Example: I imagined worst-case scenarios rather than staying realistic.

_____

_____

_____

Is it possible to not be perfect and still be a success? Circle one answer: YES   NO

The Bottom Line: **Mistakes are part of being human.**
Give up needing to be perfect.

relax the pressure you put 30
on yourself and others

idea

Pressure is a feeling of heaviness that you put on your own shoulders, which weighs you down. A typical thought is, "I'm so stressed out." We often place demands on others, and ourselves with terms like "need to," "have to," "ought to," "must," or "should," all of which escalate pressure. The real problems arise when our demands are unmet because believing that any expectation must be met leads to feelings of frustration and anger. You can reduce stress by learning to change demands into preferences.

Hannah, Phil, Eli, and Ali

Hannah believes she should give up all of her after-school activities so she can succeed academically. She thinks her friends ought to understand this and stop asking her to do social things.

Phil thinks he must start every game, that his teammates should support him, and that his parents should understand how important football is to him and stop nagging him about chores.

Eli believes he has to work out every day and worries when he thinks there won't be any time for it. He thinks his friends should stop razzing him for this.

Ali thinks she must be a size smaller than she is and thinks her parents have to stop trying to get her to eat.

When their demands are thwarted, Hannah, Phil, Eli, and Ali all experience frustration, annoyance, and even anger.

your turn

Do you feel stress and pressure from the demands you place on yourself and others? In what ways do you use the words "should," "need to," "have to," "ought to," and "must"? Write down the demands you place on yourself and others.

Examples:

My parents should let me keep my phone on all night.

My parents must let me hang out with my friends after school.

My teacher needs to stop giving us crazy amounts of homework.

I have to make varsity.

I ought to be able to eat what I want.

I should have gotten the part I wanted in the play.

Write your demand statements below.

I should… _____

I must… _____

I need to… _____

I have to… _____

I ought to… _____

I should have… _____

more practice

By replacing demands with preferences, you can remove unnecessary pressure by replacing anger, annoyance, and frustration with neutral acceptance. Instead of "should," "must," "need to," "have to," "ought to," or "should have," consider trying the following:

It would be nice if... _____

I would prefer that... _____

I would like to... _____

I wish that... _____

Example: Instead of thinking, *My parents should let me keep my phone on all night*, try thinking, *I wish my parents would let me keep my phone on all night.*

Does the anger, annoyance, or frustration decrease when you replace a demand with a preference? Circle one answer: YES   NO

For each demand statement you wrote down earlier, replace the demanding word with a preference from this list and see how it impacts you.

Revised Non-Demanding Statement	Impact

This week, take demand statements out of your vocabulary and replace them with preference statements: "It would be nice," "I would prefer," "I would like," and "I wish."

The Bottom Line: Reduce pressure by replacing demands with preferences.

reduce upset from unmet 31 demands

idea

Anger comes from the demands you place on yourself and others that are unmet. The real upset comes from the meanings you derive when your expectations are not met. When that happens, you wonder what it means to you and what it means about you or the other person. These meanings create unpleasant feelings, such as hurt, sadness, anxiety, and fear. A helpful way to diminish unnecessary upset is to learn to identify and question the meanings you impose on unmet demands.

Frank

Frank thought he should be able to go to a concert with his friends on Thursday night. But his parents told him that he couldn't go and he feels angry. He thinks they are saying no because they don't trust him and assume he will be pressured into doing something dangerous and illegal. This makes him sad because he has never done anything to warrant that. He fears his parents will never let him do the things other kids get to do.

your turn

Think back to times your demanding "should" statements didn't happen and see if you can identify what each meant to you, or about you.

Demanding "Should" Statement	Meaning	Emotions
Example: *My friend should not have just stopped texting me back.*	*She is blowing me off because she doesn't care about me.*	*I feel hurt and sad.*

more practice

Use your questioning skills to evaluate the accuracy of a meaning you gave an unmet expectation. Remember to consider all the possible explanations, look for the facts, see the big picture, and come up with alternative explanations. See if your new view affects how you feel.

Example

Demanding "Should" Statement: My friend should not have just stopped texting me back.

Meaning: She is blowing me off because she doesn't care about me.

Emotions: I feel hurt and sad.

Alternative Viewpoint: The fact is that she has been a good friend to me for a long time. She usually answers my texts and tells me when she has to do something else. It's not typical of her to just stop texting, maybe something else is up. I guess she might have lost service, or her phone died, or she is somewhere where she can't use her phone. She probably wasn't blowing me off. I can't let this mean more than it does.

New Emotions: I feel more neutral about it and less hurt.

Demanding "Should" Statement: _____

_____

Meaning: _____

_____

Emotions: _____

Alternative Viewpoint: _____

_____

_____

_____

New Emotions: _____

Demanding "Should" Statement: _____

_____

Meaning: _____

_____

Emotions: _____

Alternative Viewpoint: _____

_____

_____

_____

New Emotions: _____

Demanding "Should" Statement: _____

_____

Meaning: _____

_____

Emotions: _____

Alternative Viewpoint: _____

_____

_____

_____

The Bottom Line: **Don't jump to conclusions just because your expectations weren't met.**

32 relax the parent pressure

idea

You might feel pressure coming from your parents; this pressure can be unintentional, created from your own imagination, or real.

Unintentional pressure often comes from parental concern. To ease their worry, parents ask endless questions and check in on every sphere of your life. It's also possible that they just want to feel connected and are simply asking about your day.

Imaginary pressure is when you think you can read your parents' minds; you imagine that your parents think you should be trying harder, doing better, or doing more.

Real pressure is when your parents place demands on your performance. They say demanding should statements, such as "You should be studying," "You should start thinking about college," and "You should have gotten a better grade."

Whether the pressure is unintentional, imagined, or real, you can learn to take charge and not let parent pressure get the best of you.

Cole and Carson

Cole's parents constantly ask him how he is doing in school, how he did on his latest exam, and how he performed on the field. Cole feels pressure to do well and thinks his parents expect him to always do better, or else they wouldn't keep asking. Cole's parents, on the other hand, think he is doing just fine and, in fact, think his achievements are pretty awesome. They keep asking because they want to feel connected to his life. The pressure from Cole's parents is unintentional and mostly in Cole's imagination.

Carson also thinks her parents put a lot of pressure on her to do well in school and on the field. When she gets home from practice, her mom is like a helicopter circling around her, telling her what to eat, nagging her to get right to work on class assignments, and staying on her to make sure Carson puts in extra time and effort. Her mother checks the parent portal for class updates and grades, and she talks about little else. Carson's dad focuses on her field hockey performance and spends a lot of time talking to coaches, maneuvering to pave the way for Carson to gain a spot on a college team. The pressure Carson feels is real.

The pressure both Cole and Carson feel leads them to doubt themselves and wonder if they will ever live up to their parents' expectations.

your turn

Almost all parents place expectations on their kids, wanting them to succeed and be happy. Excessive pressure is the problem. Do you think your parents place unreasonable pressure on you? This chart will help you uncover how you think your parents pressure you and examine if the pressures are imagined, unintentional, or real. Use it to write down what your parents expect from you and record how you know this. Then ask yourself is the pressure unintentional, imaginary, or real.

Activity	Parents' Expectations	What Led You to Believe This	Unintentional, Imagined, Real, or Don't Know
School			
Sports, music, arts			
Extracurricular activities			
Volunteering, work, job			
Social life			
Chores			
Other:			

Now think about how these unintentional, imagined, or real parent pressures affect you. Do they affect how you think about yourself, feel, and choose to behave? Record the impact in the exercise that follows, using the example provided as a guide.

Example:

> *Every day, Tony gets home from school already stressed out because of the amount of homework he has ahead of him. He heads to football practice and at seven o'clock, he finally sits down to dinner. Rather than relaxing, he finds himself tensing up even more.*

The pressure Tony feels from his parents leads him to…

Think: Here we go. They're going to ask about my day. It's the daily parent inquisition. If I tell them I don't think I did well in math, then they'll ask me a million questions about it and make it seem like I didn't study enough, read the instructions carefully enough, or go to my teacher for extra help.

Feel: Annoyed and irritated.

Behave: Give one-word answers and eat as fast as I can so I can go to my room.

Did his parents' expectations lead him to conclude something about himself?

Doubt Label: I fall short.

The pressure you feel from your parents leads you to . . .

Think: _____

_____

_____

Feel: _____

Behave: _____

_____

Do your parents' expectations lead you to conclude something about yourself?

Doubt Label:

_____   _____   _____

more practice

Regardless of the unintentional, imagined, or real pressure your parents place on you, what matters are the reasonable goals and expectations you set for yourself. Ask yourself what you want to gain from your activities. Then write down the reasonable expectations you can put on yourself and then see if they match your parents' expectations.

Activity	Your Realistic Expectations for Yourself	Do Your Expectations Match Your Parents' Expectations?
School		Circle one answer: YES NO SOMEWHAT
Sports, music, art		Circle one answer: YES NO SOMEWHAT
Extracurricular activities		Circle one answer: YES NO SOMEWHAT

Activity	Your Realistic Expectations for Yourself	Do Your Expectations Match Your Parents' Expectations?
Volunteering, work, job		Circle one answer: YES NO SOMEWHAT
Social life		Circle one answer: YES NO SOMEWHAT
Chores		Circle one answer: YES NO SOMEWHAT
Other		Circle one answer: YES NO SOMEWHAT

Now think about how setting realistic goals and expectations for yourself can affect how you view a given situation. Does it affect how you think about yourself, feel, and choose to behave? Record a situation—either one that didn't go as you'd have liked or one where the outcome was unknown—and then note the effect parent pressure had on your thoughts, feelings, and behaviors. See if any doubt label was activated.

Example

Situation: I took a math test and thought I did pretty well.

My own realistic expectations lead me to…

> **Think:** *I did well in math for me. Math is not my best subject. I'm happy that I completed all the problems and knew how to solve a decent amount of them, was fairly sure on some of them, and gave my best guess on the rest of them.*

> **Feel:** Calm

> **Behave:** I chilled out and moved on.

Do your expectations lead you to conclude something about yourself?

> **Doubt label or self-confident belief:** I'm capable.

Situation: _____

_____

My own realistic expectations lead me to...

Think: _____

_____

_____

Feel: _____

Behave: _____

_____

Do your expectations lead you to conclude something about yourself?

Doubt label or self-confident belief:

_____   _____   _____

What did you learn? Regardless of your parents, you can be in charge of what makes sense for you. Instead of feeling frustrated, angry, upset, or anxious, don't let the outside pressure take over. Instead, let the reasonable goals you set from within be your guide.

The Bottom Line: **Relax the parent pressure by setting your own reasonable goals.**

deal effectively with 33
outside pressures

idea

Unrealistic expectations add pressure to your already busy life. There is a lot required of you on a daily basis. Your days are super full with school classes, homework, studying, clubs, leadership activities, fine arts, athletics, socializing, home responsibilities, and perhaps a job. Realistic expectations are appropriate in everyday activities that you routinely perform to help you stay current. Adding on unrealistic expectations—which are the demands you put on yourself or others or that others put on you—drives your stress level all the way up.

Ben and Amanda

Ben heard on the news that some kid got into every Ivy League school in the country, and he feels he should be able to do the same. His teachers told him that if he only did more work, his grades would be stronger. And a school committee Ben is on pressured him to do more as well. Ben thinks the world is telling him he is falling short and should be doing more.

Amanda scanned the magazines in the pharmacy and couldn't imagine herself looking good in any of the latest fashions. Her lacrosse coach expects her to be captain in the spring season and her guidance counselor is pushing her to stay in honors French. Amanda feels the pressure to do more but is too overwhelmed by it all to keep up.

your turn

What are the outside pressures you experience? Where do they come from?

Example

You feel pressure to: Join more clubs

Pressure comes from: Friends and guidance counselor

This pressure makes you...

   Think: *I can't handle it all. I'll never have time to get my homework done.*

   Feel: Stressed

   Behave: Go to club meetings and stay up extra late doing work

   Believe: I'm a stressed-out basket case.

You feel pressure to: _____

Pressure comes from: _____

This pressure makes you...

   Think: _____

   _____

   Feel: _____

   Behave: _____

   Believe: _____

more practice

For each outside pressure you listed, think about whether what you imagine, or know, others are asking from you is what you want for yourself. Notice if you think any of the following: *I have to live up to this pressure, I would like to live up to this pressure,* or *I prefer not to take on this pressure, as it is their agenda and not mine.* Then add your comments to that column. (If you need more space, download a worksheet version of this chart from http://www.newharbinger.com/34831.)

State the Pressure	I Have to Live Up to This Pressure	I Would Like to Live Up to This Pressure	I Prefer Not to Take on This Pressure
Join the business club			*I'm not joining this club just because my friends are. I'd rather spend the time doing the Model UN and Spanish Club. I don't have time to do all three.*

Look back at what you wrote in the chart. If you demand that you live up to outside pressure, be sure to acknowledge that the outside pressure and your own are in sync. If not, state that. Be in charge of the actions you take.

The Bottom Line: **Don't give in to outside pressure. Make your own choices.**

Part 8

Confidence Skills at Work

34 effectively deal with messing up

idea

At one point or another, everyone makes mistakes, uses poor judgment, or simply messes up. You can strive to never mess up, but expecting that you will never blunder is unrealistic. Don't let one error snowball into an avalanche of trouble or come to define your character. Before you do something risky, illegal, inconsiderate, inappropriate, or wrong, think about the negative consequences that could follow.

Still, sometimes, despite your best efforts, you might make the wrong choice. When you do mess up, you can learn to effectively deal with the problem by: taking responsibility for your action; clearly communicating why you understand it was an error; gaining experience by learning from it; and becoming clear that, moving forward, you won't make the same mistake again.

Omar

The soccer and football coaches turned a blind eye when boys urinated in the fields before a game. So Omar thought nothing of using the same field to urinate during an activity period in class. At some level, he knew it was wrong, but he also thought it was no big deal to the school. A teacher spotted him and before he knew it, he was sitting in front of the vice principal getting reprimanded. Omar made a joke out of it and halfheartedly apologized. When asked to give a reason why he shouldn't be suspended for this behavior, Omar simply shrugged his shoulders. This escalated the vice principal's anger, and Omar left his office with a three-day suspension.

your turn

There are two paths to take when you mess up. The first is to get defiant, defensive, or apathetic. The second is to effectively take charge of the situation in order to maximize your recovery from it. Read through this example, thinking about which of the options you would normally favor—and where that option might lead.

During a test, you are caught looking at another student's answers and sent to the vice principal's office. He threatens to suspend you.

Your response is to…	
Stay calm and use a soft, clear voice	Get angry and use a loud voice or mumble
Acknowledge what you did	Get defensive, make excuses, or deny that you messed up
Apologize for your behavior	Halfheartedly apologize or don't apologize at all
Assure him that you will not make this mistake again	Don't assure him of anything and say nothing
Plead for mercy and try to negotiate a reasonable punishment that is less severe	Shrug your shoulders, or smirk

While it's true that both sets of options may lead to the same result, the path outlined in the left column has more potential for a better outcome. The path on the left shows the person you wronged that the problem is as important to you as it is to him or her. Even when you think the mistake isn't a big deal, it is essential to acknowledge the other person's viewpoint as a sign of respect. Assuring the person that you will not make the same mistake again and that you will try your best next time lets him or her know you are taking this seriously. The mature path requires you to be willing to take responsibility for what happens and not let your mistakes compromise your future.

more practice

Think of a time you got yourself into trouble. For example, you may have lost your temper with your parents, broken a school rule, gotten into a fight, posted something mean on social media, cheated on a test, or neglected to do something important.

Describe the way you messed up: _____

_____

Once you were in trouble for messing up, did you stay calm and speak in a soft, clear voice?

    Circle one answer: YES   NO

Did you acknowledge what you did and that you messed up? Circle one answer:
        YES   NO

If not, what did you do instead?

_____

Did you apologize for your behavior? Circle one answer: YES   NO

If not, what did you do instead?

_____

Did you assure an authority figure or the person you wronged that you would not make the same mistake again?

    Circle one answer: YES   NO

If not, what did you do instead?

_____

Did you plead for mercy and try to negotiate a reasonable punishment that was less severe?

Circle one answer: YES   NO

If not, what did you do instead?

_____

What can you conclude about the way you handled getting into trouble?

_____

_____

Did you effectively deal with messing up? Circle one answer: YES   NO

Are you now aware of how you could have dealt with the situation more effectively?

Circle one answer: YES   NO

The next time you face a situation in which you get yourself into trouble, remember these strategies so you can effectively deal with it.

The Bottom Line: **Don't make more of a mess when you mess up.**

35 don't be defiant

idea

Most people don't want to be told what to do, think, or feel, but for you, as a teen, this might be exceptionally bothersome. The strong feelings that arise include anger, irritation, frustration, or annoyance and are often linked to thoughts of powerlessness or helplessness. These feelings and thoughts can make you believe that you are being manipulated or controlled. In a state of defiance, you might do the opposite of what is being asked of you, or you might become argumentative and unwilling to agree to anything. This deliberate defiance can work against you. Instead of helping you effectively take control of the situation, get what you want, and act in your best interest, oppositional behavior gets you into trouble, takes away your power, and comes with negative consequences you would rather avoid.

Brian

Brian was two weeks into his monthlong senior internship when his supervisor gave feedback that he was not performing as expected. He was coming in late, leaving early, and rarely completing tasks. In addition, his teacher told him that if he missed another history class he would flunk and therefore fail to graduate. Brian didn't understand why his supervisor and history teacher were making a big deal out of what he thought were unimportant things. He responded by thinking, *I should be able to do what I want*. The truth was, Brian really wanted to graduate, and pass both history class and the senior project. The last thing he wanted was to repeat either of those experiences. But instead of complying by showing up for class, getting to his internship on time, staying all day, and doing what they asked of him, he refused to cooperate. He wound up in the worst situation possible: forced to redo his internship and attend summer school, he lost the very freedom he desired so much.

your turn

Are you defiant? Take this quiz to find out. Circle one answer to indicate whether these statements are true or false.

1.	You hate being told what to do.	True	False
2.	You are usually compliant when someone in authority asks something reasonable of you.	True	False
3.	You do the opposite of what is being asked of you, regardless of the consequences.	True	False
4.	Before you agree, or don't agree, to do what is being asked of you, you think about the consequences.	True	False
5.	You equate yielding to the demands of others with being weak, helpless, or powerless.	True	False
6.	Working within the guidelines of what is expected by authorities gives you power and shows your strength.	True	False
7.	You argue against every viewpoint, even if you actually agree with what has been said.	True	False
8.	You are willing and able to see different viewpoints and acknowledge when someone else is right.	True	False
9.	You are usually oppositional and argue against doing what is asked of you.	True	False
10.	You usually do what is asked of you without argument.	True	False

How many odd-numbered statements were true? _____

How many even-numbered statements were true? _____

If you circled "True" for more odd-numbered statements, then you are defiant. Be wary of your tendency to do the opposite of what is asked. Instead, ask yourself what you really want and weigh which choice will get you closer to that. Try being compliant and see what happens.

more practice

The next time someone asks you to do something, try actually doing it and see if it pays off. Record your experience here.

Describe what you were asked to do: _____

_____

Despite your inclination to resist, just do it.

What was the outcome?

_____

_____

Did complying get you closer to what you wanted in the long run?

_____

_____

The Bottom Line: **The next time something reasonable is asked of you, comply and realize your power.**

dampen the judgment 36

idea

Dampening judgment to effectively cope with life's problems is a three-step process consisting of acknowledging a distressing situation, accepting it, and figuring out the effective action to take. More specifically, the first step is to acknowledge the facts of a situation. The second step, acceptance, is the most critical because acceptance allows you to remove biased, negative judgments. It helps you observe unpleasantness, problems, or difficulties without imposing meaning on situations. These meanings we impose can be conclusions we draw about others, consequences, or ourselves that are untrue or imagined. Acceptance is a clear, objective view of the facts without negative judgments, and it enables you to take the third step toward coping with life adversity, which is to take appropriate, effective action.

Julie

Julie got her first speeding ticket. She immediately hid it away, fearing that the wrath of her parents would lead them to assume she was an irresponsible driver and take her driving privilege away. She kept the speeding ticket hidden well past the due date, so a second notice arrived at her home with an additional fine imposed for late payment. Julie's failure to acknowledge the problem, the meaning she imposed on her parents, and her ineffective action all resulted in even worse consequences.

your turn

Practice choosing the effective path by considering this situation. Imagine you missed your good friend's party. Do you let the situation get the best of you? Or do you dampen the judgment and cope? Which path would you take?

Step 1: Acknowledge

Ineffective Path	Effective Path
Pretend that you went to the party	Face your friend's disappointment
Fail to acknowledge your absence	Acknowledge your absence from the party

Step 2: Accept Without Judgment

Ineffective Path	Effective Path
You think: *This will be always held against me.* *I will be excluded from the inner circle from now on.* *I may lose friends over this.* *This is one more reason for her not to like me.*	You think: *I accept my friend may be disappointed and even upset with me, but there is no reason to think this is going to have lifelong consequences or that it will compromise my friendships.*

Step 3: Effective Action

Ineffective Path	Effective Path
Avoid your friend	Face your friend
Avoid talking about the party	Apologize for your absence, regardless of the reason

more practice

Try dampening the judgment to effectively cope with difficult situations, problems, and challenges. This week, practice acknowledging, accepting, and choosing effective action.

Describe a problematic situation: _____

_____

How did you acknowledge it?

_____

_____

How did you accept the situation without judgment?

_____

_____

What effective action did you take?

_____

_____

_____

You can download additional copies of this exercise, if you need them, at http://www .newharbinger.com/34831.

The Bottom Line: Cope by acknowledging, accepting, and choosing effective action. Don't judge.

recognize realistic concern

idea

When a worrisome thought crosses your mind that creates a feeling of anxious distress, the first question to ask yourself is whether the concern is real. Realistic concerns anticipate potential problems or may be warning you that you are not fully equipped to face a difficult situation that's occurring now. The anxiety you experience is a good thing, because the alarm it sets off inside you prepares you to face the difficult situation in the best way possible. Appropriate actions in the midst of realistic concerns may include thinking through situations, examining your options, and coming up with plans and then acting on them. Self-doubts creep in when you imagine dangers that aren't really there or are unlikely to happen, or exaggerate consequences. And they stop you from feeling that you can cope effectively. Self-doubts blind you from seeing yourself as a resource and from recognizing the outside help that is available.

Kira

Kira was invited to go on a ski trip with her friend's family. Her first thought was concern about her ability to keep up with them on the slopes. Kira is not an experienced skier, and she knows the rest of them have been at it their entire lives. Knowing her concern was realistic, Kira shared it with her friend, who confirmed that Kira would be on her own on the green slopes. In a separate situation, Kira was invited to join her friends for an afternoon of go-karts and miniature golf. She had a big paper due and feared she would never get it done if she went. But the truth was that Kira had plenty of time to complete her work and was constantly turning down her friends. It was starting to negatively affect her relationships.

For Kira, self-confidence helped her assertively confront her friend about her realistic concerns about skiing, while self-doubt about her ability to finish her homework inappropriately kept her from seeing her friends.

your turn

This quiz can help you learn to tell the difference between realistic concern and self-doubt. In the two examples below, which response is which? And what is the reasonable action?

Someone offers to sell you a fake ID so you can go see your favorite band at the local bar.

A. You decline the offer, knowing you will probably get turned away at the door, that your ID will be confiscated, and there might be legal consequences for trying to use it.

B. You take your chances, buy the ID, and go to the concert.

C. You wish you had the courage to say yes, but decline the offer, thinking you are a wimp.

You and your friends see an opportunity to climb a fence and enjoy a late-night swim at a swimming pool that has closed for the day.

A. You speak up and say that, although it would be fun, you think it's a bad idea knowing the trouble you all could get into.

B. You leap onto the fence without a second thought.

C. You make a lame excuse, thinking how much of a baby you are.

In both examples, option A conveys realistic concerns. There were real possibilities of danger.

In both examples, option B presents ignorance of realistic threats and put you in harm's way. It was not a reasonable action.

In both examples, option C results from self-doubt. Instead of recognizing the realistic concerns that led you to decline the offers, you believe your self-doubt.

In the two examples below, which response conveys unrealistic, imagined, or exaggerated concern, and which reflects self-confidence? What is the reasonable action?

The semiformal dance is approaching and you would like to invite a friend from another school to be your date.

A. You imagine being turned down and think nothing could be worse than rejection.

B. You don't want to risk the rejection, so you don't ask.

C. You know it's possible your friend could say no, for all sorts of reasons, but you take the chance because you know that wouldn't be the end of the world.

Your history teacher has assigned a short PowerPoint presentation in front of the class.

A. You imagine messing up and, as a result, believe everyone will think less of you.

B. You don't want to face the scrutiny, so you stay home sick on the day your presentation is scheduled.

C. You realize how prepared you are for the assignment, know you can communicate the message to one person and to a crowd, and volunteer to go first.

In both examples, option A conveys unrealistic concerns. You exaggerated the probability of, and consequences for, an imagined threat.

In both examples, option B describes unreasonable actions. You let imaginary danger get in the way of your goals and what you wanted.

In both examples, option C represents self-confidence. Instead of letting unrealistic concern color your perspective, you chose reasonable action.

more practice

The next time a concern crosses your mind, before you leap into action or withdraw, think through whether that concern is realistic or coming from doubt. Here are a series of steps you can follow to do this.

Step 1: Label the situation that triggered your concern. Examples include: starting a new job, giving a speech in class, taking a test, accepting a social invitation, and leaping on an opportunity to do something.

Step 2: Ask yourself whether there is cause for realistic concern or if self-doubt is operating. The following questions will help you determine a realistic concern.

- Do I have the experience or skills that I need?

- Is there a resource outside of myself that can help me face this situation?

- Is the threat an unlikely possibility, or is it more than likely to happen?

- If something bad happened, would the consequences be significant?

Step 3: Take reasonable action. Consider what action you can take that would get you closer to your goals and would obtain what you want without putting your well-being in jeopardy.

The Bottom Line: **Know the difference between realistic concern and imaginary self-doubt.**

idea

Worry consists of persistent, nagging thoughts—it can even feel like you are obsessing about something. You think about things that have already happened that you cannot change or things that may happen in the future. Thoughts that worry about the future may take the form of "what-if" scenarios, worst-case situations, or awful consequences. Worry creates a lot of unnecessary emotional and physical distress. It puts your body on high alert, because you fear impending danger. Worry serves no purpose and instead steals energy, fatigues you, exacerbates pain, interferes with sleep and eating, increases muscular tension, isolates you, and keeps you from enjoying the present moment. Don't waste your time with delaying, limiting, or setting a time to worry. Work on eliminating it completely. You will stop worrying if you can accept that should a real problem arise, you will get through it.

Sam

Sam has been having trouble sleeping. Every night as bedtime approaches he worries he will not be able to sleep. Instead of focusing on a book or paying attention to the television, he thinks, *What if I can't sleep, what if I can't sleep, what if I can't sleep?* Dwelling on the fear of not being able to sleep leads him to worry more about all the terrible consequences of not sleeping, such as feeling awful the next day, being unable to function in school and on the field, and being dull to hang around with.

your turn

Name a worry you have had recently, such as the following: "What if I don't do well on my test?"; "What if he doesn't call me back?"; "What if I get a low score on my college entrance exams?"; "What if I don't have a date for prom?"; "What if my cold doesn't get better?"; or "What if I get a big pimple right before my senior picture?"

Describe your worry: _____

_____

How did it affect you emotionally, physically, and behaviorally?

Emotional examples: fear, sadness, anger, anxiety

_____

Physical examples: chest discomfort, stomach distress, dizziness, sweating, muscular tension

_____

Behavioral examples: pacing, inability to sit still, shaking

_____

Did worry block you from achieving a goal or getting something you wanted?

   Circle one answer: YES   NO

If you want to do this exercise with other worries, you can download a worksheet for this exercise at http://www.newharbinger.com/34831.

more practice

Here is a process you can follow to replace a worry with problem solving.

State your worrisome thought here: _____

_____

Ask yourself, is the worry is a remote possibility, or likely to happen?

_____

STOP HERE if the worry is a remote possibility. Continue to the next question if it's likely to happen.

Define the real problem, as specifically as possible: _____

_____

What is the worst thing that could happen?

_____

_____

STOP HERE if the worst thing that could happen is fairly insignificant. Continue to the next question if what might happen feels like a big deal.

If the worst thing happened, could you cope?

_____

_____

If what you are concerned about is more than likely to happen and would be a significant problem, what options do you have to take care of it? List them and look at their pros and cons. _____

_____

_____

_____

Can you deal with the situation now? Later? Or is it something that is out of your control?

_____

_____

STOP HERE if the problem is out of your control or there is nothing you can do. Continue to the next question if there is something you can do.

What appropriate action can you take?

_____

_____

_____

Use this process every time you start to worry. (There's a worksheet version of this exercise available at http://www.newharbinger.com/34831, if you find it useful.) Facing a real problem and trying to address it is not the same as worry! Remember that the goal is to turn off worry and to problem solve whenever you can.

The Bottom Line: **Don't let worry rule you, let it go.**

don't procrastinate

idea

Procrastinating is putting things off until the last minute, and it can wreak havoc in many spheres of your life. Whether it's failing to get work done, missing a deadline, losing out on an extracurricular activity, or avoiding work or social opportunities completely, the results are often the exact opposite of what you wish for and truly want. Regardless of what drives your procrastination, you can overcome it by learning to face tasks head-on. Three principles can help this happen: 1) action comes before motivation, which means you can begin acting without wanting to, feeling like it, or even having the energy to do it; 2) success is in the doing and not the outcome, which means participation and effort are what truly counts and the outcome is only a bonus; 3) failing to give yourself credit for your accomplishments diminishes your ability to break the procrastination habit.

Stephanie and Scott

Stephanie put everything off: her schoolwork, eating, returning phone calls, chores, and even sleep. The tasks on her plate felt overwhelming and she didn't know where to start. One night, she was sitting at the kitchen table well after midnight, struggling with a history paper. It was due the next day and she realized how stressful her procrastination makes her life feel. As a result, Stephanie felt inadequate and wondered how she would ever manage.

Scott knew he was a procrastinator but didn't care, even though the bad habit regularly led to missed due dates. Now he faces the reality that he might not graduate on time.

your turn

You can organize your time and prioritize your tasks to overcome procrastination. Here's how to get started.

Make a list of all the tasks you have been putting off or that you regularly avoid doing.

_____   _____

_____   _____

_____   _____

Assign each task a number that indicates its priority level in the list, with number 1 being the highest priority.

Step 1: Set a goal. Which task was your top priority? This is now your top goal.

_____

Step 2: State at least five reasons why it makes sense to achieve this goal.

_____

_____

_____

_____

_____

Step 3: Get organized and make a plan. Describe what you are going to do, where you are going to do it, and when you will act to make your plan happen.

What action you will take: _____

_____

Where you are going to do it: _____

_____

When you will act: _____

_____

If step 3 fails to happen, reschedule and follow the clear plan you have in place. Remember that action comes before motivation, so you don't have to feel like doing something to do it. Just take action.

Step 4: Take credit. Acknowledge what you achieved, and give yourself credit. Remember that it's the doing and the effort that count most.

You might want to do this with the other tasks on your list of priorities. If so, you can download a worksheet of this exercise at http://www.newharbinger.com/34831.

more practice

When it comes to beating procrastination, your thoughts are your biggest obstacle. "Give up" thoughts interfere with your goals by making you give up working on them, sabotaging your success, and fueling procrastination. Here are some examples of "give up" thoughts: "I'll do it later," "It can wait," "I'll do it tomorrow," "I don't feel like it," "I'm not up for it." "It's too complicated," "It's too overwhelming," "I'm too tired," and "I need to relax first."

What are the "give up" thoughts you tell yourself when procrastination wins?

_____

_____

_____

By replacing "give up" thoughts with "go to" thoughts that are goal orienting, you can beat procrastination. "Go to" thoughts remind you of the reason you made the goal in the first place, show how action can happen even without motivation, and encourage you to make your goal happen. "Go to" thoughts are not demands like "I should," but are instead compelling statements that remind you why it makes sense to take action.

Here are some examples of "go to" thoughts: "If I put this off, I may never do it," "I have made a plan; it makes sense to stick to it," "There are lots of reasons to take action on this goal, I won't let not feeling like doing it stop me," "Action is possible, even if I am not up for it or tired," "If I break the work into small steps, it doesn't have to be complicated or overwhelming," "If I start, it may get easier as I go," "I will enjoy relaxing more if I wait until after my work is done."

What are the "go to" thoughts you can use to replace your "give up" thoughts?

"Give Up" Thoughts	"Go To" Thoughts

The Bottom Line: **You can choose to stop procrastinating and get goal oriented.**

40 reach for your goals

idea

It's time to let self-confidence define you. Recognize that you are made up of many things, including strengths, assets, smarts, interests, personality traits, physical attributes, roles, and endless other qualities. You are a unique individual. In addition to positive and neutral qualities, everyone has shortcomings. Sometimes your shortcomings are also your strengths or part of what others are attracted to, especially when viewed as endearing, funny, or vulnerable. Your shortcomings are just a small part of who you are, so learning to acknowledge and accept them allows you to gain true self-confidence. Believing in yourself is not enough. It is essential that you take your self-confidence and use it to face your challenges and reach for your goals.

Cooper

Cooper was insecure about her height. Throughout her school years, she towered over most of the boys in her grade. She never let what she believed was a shortcoming get in her way. Her bubbly personality, sharp wit, and strong academic skills made her confident in all spheres of life. Recently, her height actually turned out to be a huge advantage, as she beat out many other girls for a spot on a top college sports team. Next year, when she confidently heads out to college, she will carry her height proudly.

your turn

Solidify your self-confidence by updating your self-image. Get a picture of yourself that you really like and tape it to the mirror in your bathroom. Look at the picture every day and remind yourself of what you like about yourself. Add positive feedback you have received, accomplishments that have been recognized, or hurdles you overcame. Don't deny your shortcomings, but be careful not to let them define you. You can get started now by writing down the things you like about yourself.

_____

_____

_____

_____

_____

_____

more practice

Now it's time to put your self-confidence into action. Each time a new opportunity presents itself, go for it. If you start to second-guess yourself, take action anyway. If you want to try something new or something that makes you uncomfortable, do it. Confidence comes from the effort, not just the outcome.

Recognize the effort you are making. At the end of each day, before you go to bed, list five things that you tackled. Then give yourself credit for doing them. Don't disqualify what you write by saying it was easy, not a big deal, or that someone didn't mean what he or she said. The self-confident you is able to reward yourself for your accomplishments and to use them in bolstering an even more positive view of yourself.

End-of-Day Confidence Credit List

1. _____

2. _____

3. _____

4. _____

5. _____

The Bottom Line: **Use your self-confidence to go for it and to reach for your goals.**

Acknowledgments

It has been our greatest passion and personal mission to share CBT both professionally and personally. We are so grateful that professional audiences, supervisees, and clients have received us with so much enthusiasm and devotion. Know that we truly thank all of you for the mutually collaborative process that has allowed us to educate and serve while continuing to grow and expand our skills and knowledge.

We are so thankful that our amazing families continue to be a source of ongoing support and enthusiasm for our endeavors. Thank you to all of our terrific children: Chad, Alex, Max, Jesse, Ethan, and Carly. We owe a special thank-you to Max, whose methodical editorial help made sure our verbiage and examples were true to the youth of today. And a special thank-you goes out to our wonderful husbands, Bob and Stu, who are our sources of love and constant encouragement.

We are indebted to our amazing team at New Harbinger—Tesilya Hanauer, Clancy Drake, Jennifer Holder, Vicraj Gill, and Jesse Burson—for all the time, energy, and hard work they contributed to the making of this workbook.

Most importantly, we are so appreciative for the good fortune of having Aaron T. Beck, MD as our mentor and advocate for many a decade. The father of CBT's wisdom shines in every endeavor we take.

Leslie Sokol, PhD, is a licensed psychologist, and distinguished founding fellow, certified trainer/consultant, past president, secretary, and credentials chair of the Academy of Cognitive Therapy. A fellow of the Association for Behavioral and Cognitive Therapies (ABCT), she was past director of education at the Beck Institute for Cognitive Behavior Therapy for almost fifteen years, and is a highly acclaimed national and international lecturer. Sokol was behavioral science chair of the family practice department at Mercy Suburban Hospital for twenty-two years where she also served as staff psychologist for cardiac rehab, physical rehab, nursing home, hospice, and family practice clinic.

Sokol has been training mental health professionals in cognitive behavioral therapy for over thirty years. Her coauthored book, *Teaching and Supervising Cognitive Behavioral Therapy* is the first comprehensive text to provide effective, empirically validated training and supervision. She is also coauthor of *Think Confident, Be Confident; Think Confident, Be Confident for Teens*; and two academic edited book chapters: "Dealing with Difficult Cases" in *The Wiley Handbook of Cognitive Behavioral Therapy*, and "The Generic Model of Cognitive Behavioral Therapy" in *The Science of Cognitive Behavioral Therapy*. Sokol is published in peer-reviewed journals. Her private practice is located in the suburbs of Philadelphia, PA.

Marci G. Fox, PhD, is a licensed psychologist who has been in private practice for nearly twenty years specializing in cognitive behavioral therapy with teens and adults. She has worked with the Beck Institute for Cognitive Behavior Therapy in Philadelphia, PA, for almost the same amount of time. As an Academy of Cognitive Therapy certified trainer/consultant and adjunct faculty member at the Beck Institute, she trains individuals in cognitive therapy both nationally and internationally. She is actively involved in training thousands of mental health professionals nationally to increase their competency in cognitive behavioral therapy.

Fox has a founding fellow distinction, as well as invited placement on the board of examiners and credentials committee of the Academy of Cognitive Therapy. She has lectured for years on cognitive therapy, as well as confidence and self-esteem. She has coauthored the books *Think Confident, Be Confident; Think Confident, Be Confident for Teens; and Teaching and Supervising Cognitive Behavioral Therapy.* Fox has published in peer-reviewed journals and diverse publications in the area of cognitive behavioral therapy. Her practice is located in Boca Raton, FL. For more information, visit her website at www.thinkconfidentbeconfident.com.

Foreword writer **Aaron T. Beck, MD**, created and refined cognitive therapy over the course of his research and clinical career. He has published more than 600 scholarly articles and twenty-five books, and has developed widely used assessment scales. Beck has received many prestigious awards, including the 2006 Albert Lasker Clinical Medical Research Award for developing cognitive therapy. In 2013, he became the first recipient of the Kennedy Community Health Award from The Kennedy Forum. Beck has been listed as one of the ten "individuals who shaped the face of American psychiatry" and one of the five most influential psychotherapists of all time. He is emeritus professor in the department of psychiatry at the University of Pennsylvania, and director of the Aaron T. Beck Psychopathology Research Center. His current research focuses on cognitive therapy for schizophrenia, cognitive therapy for suicide prevention, and dissemination of cognitive therapy into community settings.